Bedtime Stories For Kids

The ultimate Collection of Meditation Stories to Help Children Fall Asleep Fast, Learn Mindfulness, and relax with the most beautiful stories about friendship

Author: Jessica Smith

By reading this document, the reader agrees that under no circumstances is the author responsible for any losses, direct or indirect, which are incurred as a result of the use of information contained within this document, including, but not limited to, — errors, omissions, or inaccuracies.

Table of Contents

The Wise Wizard

Shut your eyes and let's visualize an enchanted adventure.

Let's breathe slowly first and get relaxed, pull up the covers to your chin.

In the old, old times, in a land full of magic and mystery, there lived a magnificent King. The king was very kind and cared for all his people. He cared for all the children of his land very much too, he loved to take time out of his day to spend it with children playing outside.

The King never had children of his own. No princes or princesses. So when the time came for the King to choose the new king, the one who would take his place, he arranged a competition.

The King made the announcement that whoever opened the lock of his bedroom closet's door would become the next king!

Simple right? But there was a catch! The lock on his closet's door had no key! And they weren't allowed to break the lock...

All the young men and women of the village tried their luck, but none were successful.

In a small village of the kingdom, there lived a young boy called Sammy, and his old mother. The mother worked very hard and earned only enough money for one day's meals.

She put aside one small gold coin each day so they could visit the Wise Wizard of the mountains. The Wise Wizard could grant you any wish! But he wouldn't do it unless you brought him his favorite treat, chocolate glazed doughnuts!

By the time of Sammy's twelfth birthday, his mother had just enough money to buy seven doughnuts, seven is, after all, the fantastically magical number.

Sammy and his mother walked seven miles to the mountains, where the Wise Wizard lived in the seventh cave.

The Wise Wizard welcomed them into his dark, dusty home. Sammy wrinkled his nose but didn't utter a word, just like his mother had taught him.

Sammy's mother put down the tray of seven doughnuts in front of the Wise Wizard. The Wise Wizard picked up the first doughnut and started eating it, crumbs falling to the ground, and he munched on. Sammy cringed at sight, as he was an immaculate boy, but he didn't say anything, as he was also a boy with good manners.

When the Wise Wizard was halfway through his third doughnut, he sneezed very hard, snot drops flew everywhere! Sammy had to duck behind his mother's apron to save himself.

When Sammy peeked out from under the apron, he saw a horrible sight! The Wise Wizard was still eating the (now, snot covered) doughnut!

"Ahhh!" Sammy shouted, pointing at the Wise Wizard. The Wise Wizard stopped eating immediately. Sammy's mother looked at him in horror, she was scared that the Wise Wizard will not fulfil their wish anymore!

But the Wise Wizard said in a loud, clear voice, "I was going to grant you seven kingdoms, for the seven doughnuts that your mother brought, YOU UNGRATEFUL CHILD! But now, I will only grant you two and a half kingdoms! NOW LEAVE!"

The cave floor shook with the sound, Sammy and his mother ran out of the cave, slipped and slid down the mountain, and hurried on home.

By the time the good King announced the competition for the throne, Sammy and grown up to be a brave young man, he had entirely forgotten about the Wise Wizard and the two-and-a-half kingdoms.

One day, Sammy's mother asked him if he wanted to try to open the Kings lock. He said no he would not try it when so many other people who are smarter and stronger than him couldn't do it, then how could he? But at last, he agreed to try for his mother.

The old King smiled as he watched Sammy enter the palace, "What is your name young man?", The King asked.

"Samm- Sam! I'm Sam from the village near the mountains."
Sammy said confidently.

The King smiled more brightly, "Come and try your luck then young Sam!", he said.

Sam took a deep breath and put his hand on the lock... Oh! What's this? The lock fell into Sammy's hand!

The crowd of royal attendants cheered! The old King put his hand on Sammy's shoulder, "Congratulations, your highness!"

Sammy's mother couldn't believe it when she heard the news!

"You have been granted the first kingdom, son!" She whispered in Sammy's ear when they were alone that night. "The first kingdom?" Sammy asked, not understanding.

"The gift of the Wise Wizard!" said his mother, "The first kingdom from the two-and-a-half kingdoms he promised!" Sammy just shook his head.
It was only a month after Sammy became the king, that a neighboring country attacked Sammy's kingdom! The soldiers wanted Sammy to fight with them in the war, just like the old King had always done. But Sammy didn't know how to ride a horse! Or to hold a sword!

When all the soldiers insisted, Sammy climbed up on a horse and held out his sword. But the horse started to run away!

Now Sammy didn't know how to control the horse, so he just held on tight to the horse's reins with one hand, and to the sword with the other.

By the time Sammy's horse crossed the forest and reached the battlefield, the battle was already over, and the enemy had surrendered!

The enemy king had heard the rumor that the other king was so brave that he was riding his horse at top speed through the forest, cutting away branches in his fury! He decided they couldn't fight such a man and surrendered without a battle.

"The second kingdom!" Sammy's mother whispered in his ear when he returned to the palace. Before he could say anything in response, a messenger came to him.

The messenger was carrying a proposal for a truce from the third neighboring country, it meant that the emperor of the third kingdom had offered half of his kingdom to the Brave King Sam and requested that he didn't attack their kingdom!

And thus, Sammy received his two-and-a-half kingdoms as promised by the Wise (but a little dirty) Wizard of the mountains.

Be Grateful to Your Body

Breathe in deeply while closing your eyes. Now let that breathe came out gradually and thoroughly. Today you will learn about your incredible human body.

Relax your body, your mind. As you do it, you will feel your whole body getting cozy and calm. Your brain feels relaxed; your body feels comfortable. Everything is peaceful and perfect.

As you enjoy resting in this serene and calm state, let your mind wander freely as you hear my voice.

Think about your beautiful and incredible body, just for a moment. It does not matter what shape or size your body is, it is magnificent and beautiful. Your body is made up of unique cells, which work together harmoniously just to keep you best and perfect.

Let's think about your feet. You might have little twisted toes, or you might have perfectly straight ones, yet each and every one uniquely perfect. Your feet and toes aid you in moving and getting to wherever you want to go. You must thank your incredible feet, as that carry you from one place to another.

Now think about your legs – your incredible and long legs. Some legs are thick while some are thin, but what matters is that they are sturdy enough to help us walk and move.

It's imperative to remember that you don't need to look like anyone else. You are perfect as it is because you are YOU.

We can love and appreciate your bodies precisely as they are in real. As we age, some people whine about their bodies. They forget that all human bodies are unique and beautiful in their own particular way.

If everyone has the same bodies, it will look tedious and dull. God has made each one wonderfully. Therefore, we must always

14

remember to love each and every part of our robust and astonishing human bodies — in and out.

Consider your healthy and sturdy backbone and shoulders. They aid you in picking, lifting and moving pieces of stuff. They help you in walking and keep your body straight. You must be grateful for your firm and robust back and shoulders for holding and transferring the things you need in your life.

Now let's envision your arms and hands. How magnificent it is to be able to hug those whom you love. All because of your arms and hands, you can touch the people you care about, when they are happy and when they are sad. Be grateful to your arms and hands and admire how strong and gorgeous they are, assisting you every day in your life.

Lastly, imagine your lovely face. Your face is unique, special and unlike others. Your friends and other folks can look through your beautiful face and eyes and can perceive brilliant glow which you hold inside your heart. Even your smile can show your inner light.

Always remember to thank and admire your marvelous body, every day. It will always be with you to aid you in experiencing life and express yourself in many different whimsical ways.

Are you ready to open your eyes now?

If yes, then take a deep breath and open your eyes.

You've done an excellent job by relaxing your body, by loving your body, and finally learning to be grateful to it today.

A Big Mess

Get into the bed and snuggle in the covers.

Now take a deep breath and relax your body. Now, let breathe out the air. Are you comfortable? Good, we shall begin now!

Do you know what a forest looks like in a bright morning? A canopy of leaves filtering in the Sun's first few rays, the birds chirping their new songs for the day, dew drops sneaking past the branches to moisten the forest floor...

A girl walks by the dense row of trees, a long skirt swishing around her winter boots, a warm cloak around her shoulders, the sweet aroma of freshly baked bread drifting from the basket on her shoulder wakes up Mikey, the forest monkey.

Mikey opens his eyes and looks around, he sees the girl hurrying past him. He knows who she is, it's Sarah, the girl from the village!

Sarah carries this delicious smelling basket right through the forest every morning.

Now what Mikey doesn't know is that Sarah's family is destitute, she bakes lots of bread every morning and takes it to the town on the other side of the forest, she sells it in the bakery and brings the money home.

There's a rumor in Sarah's village that a scary old man lives in the forest. Everyone is scared of the old man. This is why Sarah always walks very fast through the woods.

Mikey always wonders what's in Sarah's sweet-smelling basket, but she walks so fast that he never gets the chance to peek.

This morning Mikey has a plan. As Sarah moves past the place where Mikey sleeps, he jumps at her feet!

Sarah screams, thinking of the scary old man, but she spots Mikey instead. Sarah had dropped her basket and some pieces of bread fall to the ground.

"Ahh, what a mess!" Sarah exclaims as she collects all her bread back in the basket and hurries away.

"A MESS," Mikey tells all his monkey friends, "It's called a MESS, Sarah's sweet basket snack!!"

"A MESS," they all shout.

Now Sarah never gives them any Mess, how will they get the sweet Mess? All the forest monkeys hold a meeting to discuss.

Steve, the baby monkey, suggests that they follow Sarah one day to see where she takes the Mess in the basket to.

Mikey volunteers to do this job.

The next morning, when Sarah hurries through the forest, Mikey hides behind a tree and watches her every step, he follows her closely, hiding behind trees and bushes.

Mikey watches Sarah give the Mess to a baker, through the glass front window of the Bakery. As Sarah walks away, Mikey enters the shop.

"Can I have a Mess?" Mikey asks the shopkeeper.

"A what? A mess?" The baker raises his eyebrows.

"Yes, yes a big Mess as big as possible," Mikey jumps up and down.

"A big mess, eh? " The baker rubs his hands together.

Mikey waits patiently as the baker goes to the back of the shop, he returns with a big plastic bag.

"Here you go, the biggest mess I have" the Baker hands the bag to Mikey.

Mikey takes the bag and leaves. But hey, what is this? The bag is hefty!! How can something as sweet and soft as Mess be this heavy?

But regardless, Mikey fulfils his duty and carries the bag with him to the forest. All the monkeys gather around the big bag of Mess. The eldest monkey opens the bag and...

A big alarm clock comes out and starts making a big scary noise.

All the monkeys get scared and run for the trees.

And to this day, you'll never see a monkey hanging out on the ground.

A Ride on a Magic Rug

Breathe in deeply and shut your eyes.

I will count down from 5 to 1, and your whole body will feel very heavy and extremely comfortable when I get to 1.

You feel so relaxed such that one might not even like to move. However, keep yourself still and relish the incredible relaxation that is about to flow into your body.

5 Feel the relaxation pouring in your arms and legs.
4 Your legs are beginning to feel heavy and your arms, too.

3 Heavier and heavier... more relaxed, calm, and comfortable

2 Relaxing more and more with each number I am saying.

1 Now your whole body is heavy, but calm and relax.

Now imagine a beautiful and colorful magic rug underneath you. This rug is the most stunning in the whole world. It has exquisite colors and is woven very neatly. Someone took great care in the making of this exceptional magical rug for you.

Reach down and feel the smooth texture of the brightly colored rug. It's very soft. Then, wrap your hands around the tassels that hang on the front corners. As you do, notice the tassels stiffen and become straight like a handle, so you can hold them and feel perfectly safe on the rug.

The magic rug starts to take off gently... making sure you feel safe and comfortable. The magic rug sways in gently form and sweeps up and then makes you giggle with so much delight!

What an adventure!

It moves you up into the thin sky, higher and higher, up to the cotton-soft clouds. It's lovely to be here as you feel completely relaxed and free. The air you take in here is clear and pure, so you take in a deep breath and breathe out it gradually.

As you exhale, your body feels perfectly bright and clear. It is all because the air around you is so clear, light and pure.

Now look below and witness the stunning green patches. It seems like the trees are waving at you as the wind blows them back and forth. As you go by, you see meadows and different crops' fields. From all the way up here, you see all the houses which look quite tiny.

You let go of your worries. You see your problems or hard feelings vanishing away. As you relax and enjoy your magic rug ride, you leave your concerns and issues far behind. This is a terrific ride.

As the rug leaps and make turns, feel as you can go as speedily as you wish, and still have more fun. Spin your body with the rug and know that you are in full control – going faster and faster or perhaps slower, as you desire. Nonetheless, you are totally enjoying your magic rug stroll.

Now, take a deep breath and when you are done, ride your magic carpet back down to the ground. Land easily and comfortably. Now bring back all the lovely, happy feelings you felt during the ride with you, then open your eyes when you're ready.

Take a deep breath and exhale completely.

Today, you did a fantastic job with your imagination!

The Golden Apple

Close your eyes firmly, and take a long deep breath. Keep breathing slowly and evenly as we begin our adventure.

Let's take a walk in a thick dark forest, leaves rustling in the wind, dried up branches crunching under our feet. Birds peeking down from high up the tree. All different colors of feathers.

Did you know some of these colorful birds, some kinds of parrots, can learn to speak human language?

A long, long time ago, there lived a King called Percy. He had a parrot just like that, one that could talk in King Percy's language. The parrot was a very dear pet of the king's, he cherished his time with this intelligent bird. The parrot also loved the king very much.

One bright day, King Percy decided to take a walk in the forest. He naturally invited the parrot to join him. And so they started to take a stroll through the thick cluster of trees, just like we had imagined earlier. The dried-up branches crunching, the breeze playing with the leaves, the birds singing.

The parrot looked around gloomily at the happy, free birds and made a request to King Percy that he had never been brave enough to make. "Your Highness, I am your very dear friend, am I not?" He began. "Oh, of course, you are, dear parrot!" The king replied without hesitation. "If I was to request something, then, it will be granted, will it not?" The parrot asked slowly, King Percy gave a chuckle, "Of course, my dear friend, ask away."

"All these happy birds, singing their hearts away, it reminds me of my home", the parrot began, "I really miss my land, my friends, the trees even. If I could just visit my land if only for a couple of days, I will be very grateful.

King Percy suddenly understood how sad the parrot must be so far away from his home, "Of course you can always visit your home! But please do return quickly, I will miss you very much."

The parrot promised to return within a month and began his journey towards his homeland.

After a month had passed, the parrot returned on a chilly morning and flew straight to King Percy. The king laughed with delight. "Welcome back my dear friend, how was your journey?", The King asked as he stroked the parrot's feathers.

"It was wonderful, your Highness", the parrot replied cheerfully, "I've brought a present for your Highness", he suddenly announced.

The court of the king all cheered in wonder, what could the parrot have brought from his land?

The parrot presented King Percy with two Golden Apples. "This is an exceptional fruit from where I come", the parrot announced with pride. "They look very wonderful", the king remarked, "But what's so special about them, can you tell?". "No, no, your Highness, that's a surprise!"

The King smiled and took a Golden Apple in his hand. But his advisor stopped him!

"Your Highness, this is a foreign fruit, we must test it first..."

The King raised his eyebrows, he handed the fruit to the advisor to test. The advisor gave the fruit to King Percy's second favorite pet, a dog.

Behold! A terrible thing happened as the dog tasted the fruit! It gave out a shrill scream and fell on his side. People were shocked, and all the angry eyes were on the parrot!

As King Percy said, "Why? My dear friend, why?", the parrot couldn't handle such shame, he fled the palace and flew back to his homeland.

In sadness and anger, King Percy made the servants throw the fruit out of the palace!

The Golden Apple landed in the soft grass of the Royal Garden, and just a little time later, a golden sprout sprang out of the ground.

Years passed, and the tiny sprout grew into a tall tree, a towering golden tree with a gold trunk and shining branches and leaves, and on the stunningly glittering branches, large golden apples grew.

No one even cared to touch the apples though, since the whole kingdom knew that the apples were venomous.

One day, a conspiring servant decided to take revenge on his cruel master by giving him a piece from the golden apples. He cut up the pieces really small and hid them in a tasty fruit salad.

The naive master ate the whole bowl without suspecting anything.

But hey! What is this? The man didn't die at all! Instead... he seemed to grow... younger... or shall we say, turn younger! The servant was shocked.

As the news reached King Percy, a wave of guilt and shame hit his heart. His dear and loyal friend really had brought him a marvelous gift. The king wrote a letter to his dear parrot friend, apologizing for how he had behaved, and urging his friend to come and meet him.

The parrot replied with a visit to that palace, and his position was once again restored as the King Percy's dearest friend.

A Fort in the Sky

Get yourself cozy and close your eyes.

Now imagine that you are the part of this story which I am going to tell you.

Take in a good deep breath, and allow the pleasant air to fill your belly up like a balloon. Now exhale all the air out.

Do this five times, so that you feel utterly relaxed.

Now imagine a Knight in shining steel armor, of course, he's not real, but I'm sure you can visualize him clearly in your mind.

He's tall and muscular and riding a magical flying horse. He gives you a helping hand you get up on the horse with him. The horse kicks its hind-legs, and you fly up, up and up.

You're soaring higher and higher, up above the clouds, soft and white around you like whipped cream on a cake.

Higher and higher and far away you fly, now you can see a fort in the sky.

The horse lands down on the fluffy white Cloud, the Knight helps you to the cloudy floor and waves you good-bye.

Now as you walk inside, the only sound you hear is the calming and crackling sound of fire in the fireplaces which warms the fort. You feel so relaxed and happy to be here.

You feel great cheerfulness and goodness in this place. You feel so blessed to be here and experience the warmth and harmony in this place.

Now, walk down the halls of this unique fort.

Note one door apparently welcoming you inside. A feeling of approval washes over you.
Peek into the room and see a really soft bed, notice your name carved on its crown. It must be a magical bed because as soon as you sit on it, it welcomes you by making you fall on it. As you lie straight in the bed, looking at the white roof above you, the soft bed washes away all your fears and problems.

It is impossible to think about anything else right now, instead of how delightful and peaceful it feels being here on the bed and watching your bad worries leaving your body. You must be feeling good from within.

Let me tell you that it is your exclusive place, and you can visit here whenever you desire. All you just have to do is to imagine and think about it.

Immediately, you feel all the stress and apprehensions reducing out from your little body. Calm and tranquil feelings engulf you. This is your special place of tranquility. It does not really matter what's happening around you, you are always welcome here to relax and feel peace and warmth.

You peacefully carry on all these feelings of immense tranquility, calmness and joy with you that fill your heart and soul this evening, while you sleep tonight.

The Grateful Turtle

Take a moment and just feel happy and grateful before we head off to sleep. Just observing what we appreciate makes our hearts feel so very full of calmness and happiness. It also bestows us with profound harmony and joy!

So, get relaxed, and when you are all set, shut your eyes.

Let your body sink into your bed. Naturally allow yourself to just relax. Take deep breaths and exhale slowly. Your body begins to relax wholly.

Envision an adorable and cuddly little animated turtle. Of course, it is unreal, but I am sure you can imagine it in your mind clearly and sharply. It can stand on its hind legs and has little turtle flippers, huge eyes, a funny crooked snout and a silly grin.

Suddenly, you notice a sparkle in its one eye!

Its name is the Grateful Turtle. Isn't he adorable?

The Grateful Turtle is here to remind us of all the things we have to be grateful for, even though we have days which sometimes are rough and hard on us.

Firstly, the happy little turtle reminds you that you woke up all well this morning. Yes! Luckily you woke up to a lovely day in your life that has many surprises and adventures for you, yet to witness. Now think, how grateful you are for simply waking up and having the chance to experience the lovely and beautiful day.

You might have learned new things today or maybe your day was just incredible. Perhaps it was difficult for you to deal with some rough stuff. But either way, you gain more knowledge today as compared to yesterday.

The Grateful Turtle reminds you that you can be grateful for all life's lessons — no matter they were pronounced or minor. To say thanks, the Grateful Turtle does a merry little dance, and you feel cheerfulness dancing in your heart.

Now, the Grateful Turtle looks at you with a glow in his eyes and smiles at your strong and robust body. You're being retold by these glow eyes of the Grateful Turtle that you moved, shifted place to place, and breathed in today. Your body really is a miracle!

You visualize your hands and feet; how active they have been throughout the day in doing all you've done.

Experiencing all the beautiful things you've witnessed today and the places you've been is all so magical. Even if you stayed home today, you have yet travelled to many places in your imagination, right? And you are grateful for all this!

Grateful Turtle does another merry little dance that makes you laugh and giggle. By doing so, it is reminding you of all the things about which you must be thankful for — all the big and small things in your life.

The Grateful Turtle reminds you of your family and friends who genuinely care for you. They love you, unconditionally, just because of who you are. You feel so right and content from within, by being reminded that you are precious and loved by many people.

Life is way better when we take time to be thankful for everything we have, and for all the things which we have learned in our life.

You should open your eyes when you're ready, and give your body a big stretch. Let yourself drift off to a peaceful sleep.

The lazy Town

There was once a town where all the people were exceedingly lazy. They clearly didn't like doing any kind of job! They didn't even clean their yards, not even their streets. Also, they couldn't get bothered with weeding their patches of vegetables.

The town was miserable; it was a shame. The chief despised it as he liked neatness and cleanliness. He would begin a clean-up operation every now and then, but only a small number of people actually turned up to offer help. Even then, they would quit working after one or two days, and the weeds would spread again, and in a matter of months, the place would again be just as bad as it was before.

One day, a strong storm blew in the town, and the place looked even worse than before once it had passed. But the worst thing was that a massive tree was blown over and thrown across the main road leading into the marketplace.

The first merchant, bringing his goods, came along and found the road blocked by a tree. He said, "I don't have all the time to move it. I have to take my products to the market. "So he walked away by walking around the tree.

Then came a second and a third trader, and did the exact same thing. No one could be bothered with doing anything about this blockage. People would come and go, look at the tree and just walk around.

The chief heard of the blocking of the road by the tree. He asked, "Why do not some of the townspeople come together and push it? "But days passed, and no one came to help, and the tree stayed where it was. The chief came up with a cunning plan to teach a lesson to his people of the town.

He took some of his servants the next morning, even before the sun had come up, and order them to dig a hole under the tree. Hiding some gold in the hole, he told his servants to cover it up again. He then made them swear that they must keep this matter a secret. Returning to his palace, he instructed his town crier to go over and summon all the townspeople to assemble at the spot of the fallen tree in the afternoon.

When they were all assembled, the chief told his people that eliminating the barrier would not take very long if all of the people worked together. One of the farmers said: "The storm put the tree there, let's ask the storm to push it out of the way.

Another lazy man said, "Yes, why should we exert ourselves if walking around it is much easier than moving and shifting it?

The Chief was frustrated. He was about to give up when a tall skinny man stepped forward. He was just a poor farmer who was all alone in the town as his all relatives were dead. "I am going to go and move that tree," he said. He soon began to pull and shift the massive tree.
The chief waited to see if anybody would come forward to help the young man, but after some time when he saw that nobody bothered to move and support the young man, he ordered his servants to help him.

The chief came to the young farmer, after the tree had been pushed to the road side , and then took him to the place that he had concealed the gold.

The chief told him to dig there, and assured him that whatever he found there will be his to keep. The young farmer began to dig and soon found the gold. He was jubilant.

The chief said to him: "This gold is all yours because you have earned it. You are free to use it the way you desire."

After that, he said to the lazy townspeople, "This is a lesson for all of you! Your laziness does not give you anything. Rewards only come to those who are willing to work hard."

Be Like a Butterfly

Take in a really nice deep breath, and close your beautiful eyes.

Let the visions and sounds of this room fade away as you focus on your breathing, and get ready to visualize a funny and relaxing adventure.

Your body starts feeling extraordinarily comfortable and slides down more wherever you are. Your legs and arms are beginning to feel very heavy. You enjoy this time patiently, as your mind and body relax.

Now, imagine you're a beautiful butterfly fluttering high in the sky. There is a lovely green valley with lots of colorful flowers under you, waiting for you to enjoy the whole scene. You feel the wind gently blowing, touching your delicate wings. As the wind blows against your body, it softly blows away your worries and stresses that you hold inside. Your mind is now clear and calm. You feel very light, just like the wind itself. You are a cheerful butterfly gliding and fluttering anywhere you wish to go.

Did you know, as a butterfly moves from flower to flower, it spreads out the seeds and pollens that are needed by other plants to thrive and grow? You are like that butterfly too. You can flutter about peacefully and beautifully — spreading kindness, happiness, and goodness wherever you go!

The sun is touching and warming your colored body. The huge puffy clouds that float in the sky remind you how relaxed and peaceful you can be whenever you desire. All you have to do is to think about it. It is incredible to feel that much light and carefree.

Your butterfly-self has left its worries or fears behind. You love how it feels to beat your wings and fly, and anytime you start to feel tired, you can land on a leaf or flower and rest. You spread your lovely wings in a big stretch. You are entirely peaceful and content as you allow your true happiness to shine through.

It's feeling so good. Your body is calm; your mind is peaceful. You can fly around as long as you want – discovering or just swirling softly on the wind.

Now inhale a deep breath and exhale gently.

When you're ready, give your body another big stretch and slowly open your eyes.

What did you like best about being a butterfly?

Keep that feeling with you as long as you can.

And remember, you can always come back here — or to any peaceful place — just by using your mind and imagination.

The Tale of the Three Brothers

Take in a deep breath and relax, today you will learn about a tale unlike any other, the ancient story of the three brothers.

Once upon a time, three brothers were travelling on a lonely winding road, at twilight. After some hours, they reached a river that was far too perilous to cross but being taught about magical spells, they simply waved their magic wands and made a bridge. Before anyone could crossover the bridge, however, they found their path blocked by a shadowy figure. It was the Death who felt cheated because travelers would usually drown and die in the river. But Death was ruthless, and he tried to pretend to compliment the three brothers on their wizardry, stating that they had each won a prize for being clever enough to avoid it.

The eldest asked for a more powerful wand than his current one, so the Death made it from the old tree that stood nearby. The second brother wanted to antagonize Death further and asked for the power to resurrect his beloved from the grave, so Death took a stone out of the river and offered it to him. At last, Death turned to the third brother, who was a humble man and enquire about what he wants. He asked for a powerful thing that would allow him to leave that treacherous place without being pursued by Death. So, the Death unwillingly handed over his own cloak of invisibility.

The first brother migrated to a remote village, where he killed a wizard with his new wand, with whom he had once squabbled. Drunk with the strength that the new wand had given him, he bragged about his invulnerability. But that night, some other wizard stole the wand and slit the brother's throat, and Death took the first brother with him.

The other brother went to his house, where he took the stone and turned it three times in his hand. To his joy, the girl he had once hoped to marry made an appearance before him. However, she soon became sad and cold because she did not belong to this mortal world. Driven insane with a desperate desire to be with his lover, the second brother killed himself, and Death took the second brother too.

As to the third brother, Death has been searching for him for many years but has never been able to find him. It was only when he reached an old age that the youngest brother shed the cloak of invisibility and offered it to his son. Then, as an old friend, he welcomed Death and gladly went with him, saying goodbye to his well-spent life.

Bubble Blower

Inhale a deep breath and close your beautiful eyes.

Imagine your belly like a balloon. As you inhale, make that belly balloon as big as you can. Now, exhale and release all the air from it.

As you breathe and relax, allow your arms and legs to get as droopy like a rag doll. Just let them get heavy and loose. They feel so massive as if you don't even want to move them because they are very comfy. Allow your body to relax continuously. Now, you will use your imaginations to paint something beautiful.

Pretend in your mind that you're pulling a huge, magic bubble blower from your pocket. It looks like a usual bubble blower, but this one has magic in it. It has been tiny in your pocket, but as you take it out, you discovered that it is going to be huge. It's greater than any bubble blower you've ever seen before.

Now, in your other hand, visualize a massive bottle of magic bubble soap. Insert the blower into the thick liquid bubble of enchantment. You may start blowing through a bubble blower to make a huge bubble. As you blow the bubble, I want you to put all of your concerns or stresses in the bubble. Good! Keep blowing the bubble until you think it's big enough. Put all of the worries in there. It will keep expanding to hold all of the concerns and stresses.

When you have done that, nod your head. (*Wait for the nod*)

As you finish blowing, visualize a strong but friendly breeze comes along and carries your worry bubble far and far away from you. It's taking it so far away that you'll never have to worry about it again. It's just leaving now. Watch it as it goes.

Doesn't it feel good to watch that worry float away? It might be gone forever. But if it comes back, all you have to do is remember that it's just a thought. And thoughts can be changed or released to help us feel better like the way we just did.

Now, you can blow up as many bubbles as you would like with your magic bubble blower. Place anything in there that worries you, and watch the wind push the bubbles away. You can use this magical bubble blower whenever you desire, all you have to do is to imagine it in your mind.

Now I'm going to be quiet so you can finish. Tell me when you're done.

Open your eyes slowly, and drift away in a deep sleep.

The Cursed Apple Garden

Pull up the covers to your chin, and breath in deeply.

Now let the air out slowly, gently.

Do you like fruits? What's your favorite fruit?
There was a King whose favorite fruit was Apple in a certain Land. He spent all his days eating apples, he wouldn't even let his dear daughter Princess Anna take any from his basket of apples.

"Anna dear, I told you the story about the Sage, haven't I?", He says every time the princess asked for an apple.

"Yes, yes Father, I know, I know, a Sage cursed the garden and anyone who eats apples from it will be abducted by a dragon, I know", the Princess replied every time, shaking her head.

One day the princess placed her clapping toy in the garden to distract the guards, but they had such intense concentration that they paid no attention to the toy.

The prince from a neighboring kingdom visited later that day. He was called the Prince Mighty. Prince Mighty was very self-centered and arrogant.

When the princess asked Prince Mighty why he was called *Mighty*, he said that it was because he was the mightiest man in the world.

The princess decided to take advantage of these traits and asked him, "Oh Mighty Prince, would you do me a favor? It would make me very happy!"

The prince readily agreed to the sweet flattery, "My dear Princess, ask as you wish!".

"I will like to eat an apple from that tree", the princess demanded sweetly, pointing towards a nearby tree.

"Oh, is that all? Well, your desire is my command, Your Highness", the prince joked as they walked towards the tree.

But the guard near the tree, a soldier called Neptune, stopped them from going any further.

"Pardon me, Your Highnesses, but I have orders from the king." He spoke very politely, but firmly.

"How dare you stop us!" The prince shouted at the soldier. The princess thought the guard was rather smart. She tried to use the situation.

"Oh please, it's just one apple I want, I have always wanted to taste one", the princess batted her eyelashes. Neptune was a kind man, he could not stop himself, "Oh my princess, only for you..." He picked an apple from a branch and offered it to her.

As soon as the princess took a bite from the apple, a giant dragon appeared from the ground and snatched the princess away before anyone could react!

As the King heard the dragon's roar, he hurried out towards the garden, shouting "Anna! My dear Princess Anna! Are you alright?" But it was too late.

When the King heard what happened, he shouted at Neptune and Prince Mighty, "The garden is cursed! I've told this to everyone who listens! I once travelled to a faraway land and stepped on a basket of apples by mistake. The basket had belonged to a sage; he had cursed me that I could only eat apples for the rest of my life. And if anyone else tried to eat an apple from the royal garden, they would be snatched away by a dragon. Oh, my dear Anna! What will I do now?"

When Neptune heard this tale, he was felt ashamed. "My king, is there no way to save the princess? I will do anything to protect her!"

The king bowed his head in despair, "Only the sage can lift the curse, but if I enter his land ever again, our own land will be burned to ashes, that was also his curse."

"I will travel to that faraway land, my King, I will rescue Princess Anna, even at the cost of my life", the brave soldier promised.

"Very well, but it's better if you were to take Prince Mighty with you. He's after all, a courageous and strong man."

"As you wish Your Highness!", The soldier replied with a bow even before the prince could respond.

And thus the two set out on their journey.

They travelled for many days, through jungles and cities, and over hills, across rivers. After a long, long journey, they reached a very thick forest.

In the middle of the forest, there was a cave, the old sage was sitting, meditating outside the cave. The soldier and the prince sneaked very quietly past the sage and entered the cave. The cave was very dark, and they couldn't see anything. Very deep in the cave, they could see a faint light.

When they reached the light, they found a horrible sight. There was a giant dragon sleeping, with its tail wrapped around the unconscious princess. "Oh, there the princess is." The prince shouted in excitement.

The dragon opened its eyes and roared. The cave shook with the force of the sound. Neptune and the prince had to run out of the cave to save themselves. They ran and ran, and took refuge under the tree.

They had been roaming for a long time; hence they were both starving. The prince took out a piece of a bun for them to share. But when they were about to start eating it, an elf appeared out of the ground.

Neptune and the prince shouted together, "Who are *you*?"

"Hello Gentlemen, my name is Elfonzo, and I'm famished! Would you gentlemen be kind enough to give me something to eat?" Neptune offered the elf his piece of the bun.

But instead of taking the bun, Elfonzo let it fall to the ground. He then asked Neptune, "Would you please pick it up for me?"

This made Neptune very angry, he said, "Shame on you if you can't even pick up a piece of the bun from the ground!"

And then, in front of their eyes, Elfonzo turned into a man. He said his name was Fonzo and he was Sage's son. One day the sage, in his anger, had turned Fonzo into an elf, and his Lea into a dragon!

The sage couldn't reverse his curses himself, but he had said that the curse on Fonzo would lift when a brave soldier will come and scold an elf under this very tree.

Fonzo answered Neptune's question before he could ask it, he said that his sister will turn back to normal when a man will sacrifice himself for the princess she had trapped.

Neptune got up without hesitation and headed towards the cave alone, he stood in front of the dragon and said in a loud, clear voice, "I am here to sacrifice myself!" He bowed his head in front of the dragon.

The dragon suddenly turned into a beautiful girl, and the princess woke up. She hugged Neptune.

After that the curse on the royal garden lifted, now everyone could enjoy the royal apples. The King, on the other hand, never ate another apple as long as he lived.

Ragdoll Relaxation

Note: Read the following lines slowly, and watch as your little ones just melt into bed for sleep.

Shut your eyes very slowly and think about a rag doll that you own or may have seen. Think about how limp and soft it is. Note all of its parts... just lying there, so happy.

When you imagine it, you can see how it hangs totally loose, limp and floppy. Assume what your body would feel like if it did the same thing. I wonder what it would be like.

Do you think you can try to make your body as relaxed as that of loose, droopy ragdoll? Just imagine doing that.

Allow your body to be as loose and as limp as a rag doll. Feel your arms go absolutely free and relax your fingers as much as you can. Enable your entire face to relax, and now turn your attention towards your back. Next, feel your forehead getting relaxed.

Now feel how your eyelids are completely relaxed as you continue to imagine that droopy stuffed toy. Now, let your belly relax. Take a deep breath slowly all the way down to your belly and note how easy it is to relax.

Note how comfortable your legs are now, too. They're feeling wholly loose and limp. They might even feel like Jell-O, so wobbly. Even your feet are beginning to feel loose and soft. It's time for all your toes to enjoy some much-needed rest along with your feet's bottoms that work very hard every day to take you to different places.

Feel how everything is too loose, soft and floppy right now — just like the stuffed ragdoll you've pictured. As you have allowed yourself to relax very well, I am certain that if I were to pick your hand up right now, your arm would probably just dive right back to your side. I'm sure that's how relaxed you've permitted yourself to be, just because it feels so good to relax our bodies.

You know, by relaxing our bodies we allow them to have some rest. Moreover, by relaxing our bodies, we can also allow our minds to relax. We can do this by allowing any thoughts to become like clouds — light and soft, drifting away slowly.

It's interesting to watch our thoughts drift away in our minds like clouds. You might notice that you feel terrific. Realize how good it feels to relax and how peaceful it is.

Take a deep breath and inhale all the peace that surrounds you. Envision that the air is filled up with lots of little bubbles of peace. Inhale all these bubbles of peace, and let it go all over your body–from head to toe. Doesn't that make you feel awesome?

Observe how your body is reacting. Every time you feel anxious or stress, or even when you just need to take some time away, you can simply imagine breathing in peace and filling your entire body with peace and happiness. You will always feel the real peace inside you –within your mind and body.

That is how strong our imagination is. If we think of something like breathing in peace, we really start to feel more peaceful. So, take a deep breath now and fill yourself with peace and joy. Now, slowly let out the air, but grab on to all the joy and peace.

You did an amazing job!

I am so proud of your use of your magnificent and powerful imagination that let you relax completely, just like that floppy ragdoll.

When you've finished relaxing, you can just open your eyes and stretch your body.

If you're ready to go to bed, you can just drift off to sleep, knowing how much you are loved and how good you really are.

The Daring Queen

Breath in slowly, fill your belly with clear air. Then, let all the air out slowly.

Relax and get all warm and cozy.

Let's get ready to go on an enchanted adventure together.

It is a tale of ancient times when lands were ruled by kings and queens. In one such land, in a royal garden, there grew a magical tree. Stunning fruits of silver grew upon it.

The garden was in the care of the old royal gardener, he spent days and nights caring for the royal garden, but especially the magical tree. Every day the old gardener woke up and collected all thirty magical fruit that grew on the tree each night.

One day, the gardener woke up to find only twenty-nine fruits on the magical tree. When he reported this to the king, the king was furious! Who could've stolen the fruit from the magic tree?

The old gardener's eldest son volunteered to guard the magical tree the next night to see who stole the magical fruit.

He stood guard by the tree and noticed every little sound. But as the clock chimed midnight, the eldest son fell asleep.

The next morning, the gardener checked the tree to find only twenty-nine fruits again. Now, the king was beyond furious to find yet another fruit missing. But the gardener's second son volunteered to guard the tree this time.

The second son guarded the tree the next night, he noticed every sound and noticed even the slightest movement. But as the night grew darker, also he couldn't resist the sleep.

When the tired old gardener checked the magical tree next morning, he got very worried, as the tree once again, had only twenty-nine fruits.

When this incident was reported to the king, he was absolutely horrid with anger, as yet another magical fruit had disappeared!

But this time, the one that volunteered to guard was the gardener's dear little daughter. In olden times, daughters were never given guard duty, it must always be sons.

But little Amelia said she could guard the magical tree better than her brothers for when her cat was a baby kitten, Amelia had always stayed awake to care for her, so she was confident that she wouldn't fall asleep on duty. And thus, Amelia was granted permission to guard the magical tree.

Amelia stayed awake the whole night, she didn't ignore a single sound, nor could any movement escape her watchful eyes. As the clock chimed midnight, Amelia finally spotted the culprit! It was a tiny silver bird plucking the fruit with its beak! Amelia took aim, but she couldn't catch the swift little thief! The only thing she caught was a shiny silver feather.

The feather was presented in the king's court the next morning. The king was shocked to discover that the culprit hadn't been caught, but he was also fascinated by the idea of a beautiful silver bird. And thus the king ordered that the bird must be found.

The old gardener's eldest son volunteered to look for the bird. He set out on the journey, and travelled through jungles, over hills, and across the rivers. On an abandoned pathway, he found an old lady carrying a big pile of firewood on her back.

"Dear young man, would you help me carry the wood," she asked the gardener's eldest son. "Get out of the way, granny! I don't have much time to waste!" The gardener's eldest son replied rudely. The old lady hunched her head and walked away.

At the end of the path, the gardener's eldest son found two houses, one very fine-looking and one very shabby. He entered the fine-looking house. The owners let him stay there for free and let him enjoy all kinds of luxuries too. He remained in that house and forgot about his poor family back home.

When the gardener's eldest son didn't return for a very long time, the gardener became really worried, so he asked his younger son to go out and look for his brother.

The youngest son set off to look for his brother. Through jungles, over hills, across rivers, he travelled. On an abandoned pathway, he also found an old lady carrying a big pile of firewood on her back. "Dear young man, would you help me carry the wood", she asked the gardener's second son too. "I'm very sorry, my dear old granny, but I'm on a quest and cannot stop to help you." The gardener's second son replied politely. The old lady hunched her head and walked away. But she turned back after a minute, and called out to the second son, "Remember dear, you will some houses at the end of that path, you should spend the night in the less beautiful one!"

At the end of the path, the gardener's second son, too, found two houses, one very fine-looking and one very shabby, just as the old lady had told him. He ignored the old lady's advice and he, too, entered the fine-looking one. The owners let him stay there for free and let him also enjoy all kinds of luxuries. He remained in that house with his elder brother, and he too forgot about his poor family back home.

When the second son also didn't return for many, many days, the gardener grew very worried again. Amelia volunteered to go look for her brothers. But her father wouldn't let her go. "I have lost both my sons already; I cannot lose my daughter too!" The gardener said. "Don't worry father, I will not get lost, I promise!" Amelia assured her father.

And so Amelia set out on her journey, through jungles, over hills, across rivers she travelled. On an abandoned pathway, she also found an old lady carrying a big pile of firewood on her back. "Dear young lady, would you help me carry the wood," she asked the Amelia. "Of course, my dear old lady! Here, give them to me!" Amelia replied eagerly. But hey! What's this? The old woman turned into a beautiful fairy, with sparkling wings and a shining magic wand!

"I was only testing you, dear girl, as I always test travelers crossing this path." The fairy explained. "Now, let me give you some special advice. At the end of this path, you will see two different houses, one very extravagant and one very shabby, you must stay the night in the shabby house, okay?" Amelia nodded in response. The fairy waved her goodbye and disappeared in a sparkly cloud.

Amelia kept travelling on the path, and at the end of this path, she found the two houses, just as the fairy had promised. Amelia remembered the fairy's advice, so she knocked on the door of the shabby house. But the person who opened the door really surprised Amelia. It was the old lady she had just met on the path. "Yes, my dear, you have recognized me as the fairy you had met earlier. I live in this village as the old woman. You can spend the night here."

The next morning when Amelia set out to find her brothers. The fairy stopped her and told her that her brothers were in the house on the other side of the street. But they will not agree to return with her to the kingdom as they have not found the silver bird that the king had sent the older brothers to look for.

She told Amelia that she knew how to find the silver bird though, but she will only tell her how to find the bird if Amelia could bring her the forest troll's three magical hair. The troll hated fairies so the fairy couldn't ask him herself. Amelia agreed to bring the forest troll's three magical hair for the fairy.

Amelia set out towards the forest troll's cave immediately. On the way to the forest troll's cave, Amelia found an old man sitting on the side of a fountain, with his head in his hands. Being the sweet, caring girl that she was, she asked him what was wrong. "My fountain was so nice, all kinds of juices flowed in the mountain, I sold the juices to feed my family, now it doesn't even give me water to drink!" He told Amelia his sad tale, "Only the old wizard of the forest can tell me the solution."

Amelia told him that she will find the old wizard of the forest and ask him this question. The old man smiled and gave Amelia a wish that she would be successful in her quest. Amelia thanked him and moved on.

On the way to the forest again, she found a little girl crying sitting next to a tree. Amelia, being the kind young lady that she was, asked the little girl what was wrong. "My daddy planted this tree when I was born, it always gives golden mangoes, we sold the mangoes and lived in peace, but now this tree grows no fruits," Amelia told the little girl that old wizard of the forest is very sage and that he would surely know the solution to this problem, she will find him and ask him. The little girl was pleased and gave Amelia a kiss on the cheek.

Amelia set out on her way again. A river separated the path she was walking on, from the forest. There was only one boat in the river, it was being towed by a very sad looking young man. He offered to help Amelia cross the river, so Amelia climbed into the boat.

The soft-hearted girl that she was, Amelia asked the man why he is so sad. He said, "I cannot stop rowing this cursed boat! I have been rowing the boat since I was a boy, I just cannot leave this work." Amelia told him about the old wizard of the forest too and assured him that she will find the solution to his problem.

He smiled as he waved her goodbye on the other side of the river.

Amelia set out into the forest to find the troll's cave. When she entered the cave, she found a terrible sight!

An old man was chained to a wall. He wore very shabby clothes and looked very sad. It hurt Amelia's heart to see him in such a poor state. Amelia went near the old man and asked him how he ended up in such a condition.

The old man told her that he was the old wizard of the forest and that the troll had imprisoned him inside the cave. He could only escape if someone tore off the troll's three golden hair.

Amelia told the old wizard that she had come to take the troll's three hair. The wizard said that the troll was terrifying, and there was no way to take his hair with force. But the old wizard knew how to make a sleeping potion, but since he couldn't move, Amelia would have to make the potion and mix it in the troll's milk jug before he came back home.

Amelia worked very fast, she prepared the drink and added it to the forest troll's milk jug. Then, she hid behind the cabinets in the kitchen.

The troll came back very hungry and tired, he just drank the milk and fell fast asleep.

As soon as the troll's head hit the pillow, Amelia plucked his three golden hair, the wizard was freed immediately.

The wizard was so happy that he told Amelia he'd give her anything she wanted! But Amelia said to him that she only needed answers to three questions!

The old wizard of the forest whispered all the answers to her. She waved him goodbye and set off on her journey back.

When she met the boatman, she told him that he should sell his boat, then he will be free from his work. The boatman was very happy and thanked Amelia.

Amelia then met the little girl sitting by the tree, she told the little girl that there is a treasure buried under the tree, once the treasure has been dug out, golden mangoes will grow on the tree again. The little girl smiled brightly and thanked Amelia.

Amelia continued her journey back. When she reached the old man and the fountain, she told the old man that there's a frog at the end of the fountain, if he took out the frog, the fountain would run again. The old man smiled brightly too and thanked Amelia.

When Amelia reached the fairy's village, she went straight to the shabby little hut and gave the fairy the forest troll's three golden hair. The fairy lighted up with delight and waved her magical wand, a beautiful silver bird in a cage appeared. The fairy handed the cage to Amelia.

Amelia took the bird and called out her brothers from the big house from across the street, they set out together towards their homeland.

The old gardener welcomed his children with tears of joy in his eyes. He hugged his youngest child, Amelia first. He was very proud of her for bringing the beautiful bird and also finding her brothers.

When the king received the bird, he was so happy that he pronounced Amelia the future Queen of the land.

As the fairy met more travelers, Amelia's adventures became more well known. By the time she actually became the queen, the people of the kingdom started calling her the Daring Queen.

A Walkthrough A Forest

Let's utilize our imaginations to discover an enchanted forest to alleviate our fears and concerns.

Close your eyes gently and breathe deeply. Do this a few times and let your body relax with each deep breath you take in. Realize how peaceful you become with this continuous deep breathing.

Note how all of your muscles tend to relax and feel good and loose. Keep breathing normally now as I guide you on this beautiful adventure... imagine walking down a very well-worn path in a magical fall forest.

The trees have made changes to all of their foliage, and now you can see an unusual combination of colors— red, gold, orange, and green.

Lots of leaves crunches under feet as one walk along the path. The air smells so fresh and crisp. Its coolness is tickling your nose and ears. It feels so good to be out here, in nature, enjoying the scenery of the fall forest.

You hear a waterfall in the distance, and you saunter towards the roaring sound of the water. You see the flowing stream as you get to the end of the path. You can see the most gorgeous white waterfall right in front of you.

It's so soothing, and it looks like moist sunshine is pouring down on big rocks. You are relaxed by the sound of rushing water. The water has to be cold since it's fall and the days are getting shorter. Soon, there might be snow too.

Sit down for some time and enjoy the stunning scenery. Listen as the water hits on the stones. Here, any pain or anxiety you have in you seemed to be washed away forever. The sound of the waterfall gushing down seems to make you calm down. It not only clears your mind but also washes away any anger and painful emotions.

Allow the sounds to wash away any worry, just let them go. Here, in this enchanted place, you will notice yourself as a calm and relaxed person.

You can go back there anytime you feel like relaxing your mind and body, and to let go of any anxiety or tension. You know, we all have problems, and often they feel stress. The only difference is that you know how to handle it.

If you want to relax and find peace, you can come here just by imagining about that kind of place and seeing yourself there.

This quiet, peaceful place by the waterfall allows you to wash away your concerns or tension at any time.

You feel lovely and rejuvenated right now. You can feel the raw energy pouring into your body and invigorating you completely. You did an outstanding job today. Now, you can just veer off into a beautiful, deep sleep for magnificent dreams and a very peaceful night.

Good night, sweet dreams.

The Unsmiling Princess

Breathe deeply and pull up the covers. Now, today it's time for a lovely little fairytale.

There once lived a princess called Rose. But there was one bizarre fact about the princess, she never laughed. She didn't even smile.

But her father loved her very much, and because he loved his daughter so much, it pained him to see her like this.

One day, he announced that whoever could make the princess smile would marry her. All clowns, jugglers, and all sorts of performers came to the palace. But, irrespective of how hard they tried, the princess never smiled.

Near the castle lived a sincere but simple and very clumsy woman named Jennifer. She lived with her mother, and they were destitute. One day, Jennifer's mother told her to go and seek work. The lady managed all she could to get a job as a helper in a workshop that stood beside the castle.

After the close of work on the first day, the owner of the workshop gave Jennifer a dozen eggs as payment, which the young woman carried in her arms, clumsy as she was.

Jennifer was so delighted that she went hurried home, running happily.

But, just in front of the castle where the princess stood at the window, Jennifer slipped, fell on the ground and smashed all the eggs. The princess could see this, but she didn't smile.

Back home, Jennifer's mother told her, "YOU FOOLISH GIRL! If you had put those eggs in your hat, you would never have broken them." "Next time, I'm going to do that mother, "Jennifer said.

The next day, after a stressful day of work, Jennifer was given a piglet as payment. Remembering her mother's words, she decided to put that little piglet in her hat and off she went towards her house.

But right in front of the castle, the piglet wiggled its way out of the hat and managed to escape.

When Jennifer ran after it, she fell into a puddle of mud and her dress got all muddy and dirty. The princess was there, watching from her window, but still, she did not smile.

As Jennifer went home dripping with mud, her mother scolded her a lot and said, "Oh Jennifer! What exactly am I going to do with you now! You didn't tie any rope to the piglet?" "I shall do that next time mother," Jennifer replied, bowing her head.

The next day, Jennifer worked even harder, so her boss decided to give her a real big fish to take home for dinner.

Just as she had promised, Jennifer tied a rope to the fish and pulled it along the road towards her home with her.

The cats smelled the fish, and they came running towards it and ate all the fish even before Jennifer could notice a thing.

This was the most hilarious sight indeed as she passed by the princess with only the spine of the fish that were tied to the rope.

The princess didn't even smile.

Jennifer's mother once again was distraught and said, "Why didn't you carry the fish, my silly girl!" "Next time, I will!" Jennifer replied, obediently.

The next day, Jennifer worked harder than ever before, and she was given a cow to take home. She then remembered the promise that she made to her mother. So, Jennifer got under the cow, lifted it onto her shoulders and tried to carry it home.

The sight was indeed the most funny of all. So, the princess was watching from the window, she laughed, laughed and laughed. She just couldn't stop laughing.

The king was delighted! He just couldn't believe it! The one to make his precious princess laugh was not a boy at all, it was a girl! A simple, poor girl!

The king realized his mistake and promised the princess could marry whoever she wanted.

And what happened to Jennifer, you ask?

She and the princess are now the best friends, and they spent the whole of their lives together.

Spring Renewal

Just read these words to your child in a relaxed way as they settle in bed for sleep or naptime.

Lie down and make your body very comfortable. Now close your eyes and start paying attention to how your breath pours in and out of your body. Don't you think it feels so lovely and soothing?

As you exhale, imagine exhaling everything that happened during the day. Imagine breathing in peacefulness. Envision tiny air bubbles containing comfort and peace of mind spreading to all parts of your body and filling you up entirely.

Right now, you feel so calm and peaceful and relaxed. Spring's coming soon. The new and exciting season is an excellent time to make way for new and beautiful things to happen in your life.

Remember that every day you grow and change! Each season brings you a new self. Think about how, in the winter months, some flowers disappear only to come back to life better in the springtime.

Imagine yourself being a flower, and ready to geminate from the bulb of the flower . You have been consistently hibernating all winter in a warm cozy shelter . The earth has protected you throughout the chilly, cold months.

So, as the spring approaches, the rains fall from the heavens, and you soak up the water thoroughly. It renews and wakes you up. Notice how you look are forward to feel the beautiful warmth of the sun again. As you break through the bulb and start growing into the beautiful, bright, proud flower that you are becoming.

This is much like how it is in life. We set new goals to strive towards and work towards all that makes us feel amazing every day. We usually make every effort to show the best and strive to be the best we can be always.

Now, think about new things that you would like to achieve or something to improve on in your life right at the moment. Are there stuffs you would like to do better? Focus on these for few moments, and imagine yourself learning, growing, and becoming better at those things. (*Pause to allow your child to imagine*).

See yourself as being perfect at whatever it is, that you wish to do. See your mind as already being real and authentic. See all the colors and all that who loves you.

You must be so proud of yourself, and everyone is also proud of what you all you have been able to achieved. Feel your happy heart because of your outputs. This is what you focused your minds on. Because of the focus and your relentless efforts to improve on a daily basis, and just as you have BELIEVED IN YOURSELF— you can make it definitely make it happen!

Just as a flower comes back stronger each and every spring, you do too. You've done a beautiful job relaxing and imagining today. When you're ready, give your body a big stretch and open your eyes.

The Lovers Who Became Butterflies

Quite a while back, in a particular piece of China, just young men were permitted to go to class. It was imagined that young ladies ought not to be taught; however, they ought to stay uninformed.

Truth be told, they were once in a while permitted out of the house, and if they went out, they ought to be joined by a male.

Zhu Ying Tai was the little girl of a well off a vendor, and she was equipped with a limitless hunger for information. She was continually scrutinizing her dad, her mom, her siblings, the workers.

She was jealous of her siblings when they began school, and she was resolved that she ought to go to class too and get training.

She irritated her folks, day in day out. They continued advising her, No, it simply isn't accomplished for a young lady to go to class, and however, she would not surrender.

They attempted to take her brain off school by getting her wonderful garments, dolls, and different toys. Nothing could deter her. The school turned into a fixation.

Her folks adored her without question, and after some time, they began to consider what they could do to fulfill Zhu's desire for learning.

The main thing they could consider was that Zhu should profess to be a kid. She could go to class if she spruced up in young men's garments!

That is the means by which Zhu at long last entered school. She didn't view it as too testing to even consider living like a kid. She was just keen on learning and scarcely ever engaged with any of her classmates after exercises.

Regardless, they thought this new kid was somewhat unusual and was very glad to disregard him. There was just a single kid she turned out to be benevolent with.

His name was Liang Shan Bo, and he was a studious youngster with delicate habits. They regularly considered together, and step by step, they turned out to be acceptable companions.

A long-time passed, and Zhu did quite well. At this point, Zhu had become mindful that her affections for Liang had become solid, past the manner in which two individual understudies would by and large feel, regardless of whether they were the best of companions.

Liang, too, felt something comparative. He couldn't exactly comprehend why he felt so firmly pulled in to this other kid.

At that point, one day, Zhu's folks send one of their hirelings with a message that she is to get back right away. The worker doesn't reveal to her definitely, other than to demand that it is her dad's desire that they return immediately.

Zhu fears the most noticeably terrible, possibly her mom is on her deathbed! So she voyages home with the hireling, and she is forcefully alleviated to discover both her folks healthy.

Be that as it may, she is stunned when her dad reveals to her the motivation behind why she has been brought home. One of her dad's business partners has a child, only somewhat more established than Zhu, and they have organized the two to get hitched.

Zhu is hopeless; presently, she understands that she is enamored with Liang, and it is him she needs to wed. Zhu then organizes the hireling to return to the school, and to ask Liang to go to the town and to take a room at a nearby hotel.

The following day the hireling returns and educates Zhu that her companion is stopping in the motel. She takes on the appearance of a kid again and goes to see Liang.

She discloses to Liang that due to a family issue, she won't have the option to return to class, yet she has a cousin who is remaining at their home.

Liang should make her associate, Zhu says she feels sure that when both of them meet, they will start looking all starry eyed at, and Liang should then approach her folks for the cousin's to submit marriage.

Zhu advises Liang to introduce himself to the house later that evening.

She returns home to change once again into her young lady's garments. She is going to fill the role of her cousin, and she feels sure that when Liang considers her to be she truly is, he also will understand that what he has been feeling for his companion this time is only love!

In the long run, her hireling comes to report that Liang has shown up, and she goes to meet her companion. She presents herself as Zhu's cousin; however, Liang is struck by the resemblance between this cousin and his companion.

Presently that Zhu at long last stands before him in with no mask, she can't control herself, and she blasts out crying and reveals to Liang the entire story of who she truly is and how much infatuated she is with him.

From the start, Liang blew up that he has been deluded, yet then he got assuaged in light of the fact that he also understands that he is truly enamored with Zhu.

Zhu then informs Liang concerning the organized marriage her folks have gotten ready for her, and they concur that he should approach Zhu's dad for her to submit marriage.

That equivalent evening, Liang requests to see the dad. Obviously, he doesn't have any thought who this youngster is. At the point when he hears that Liang needs to wed his little girl, he just snickers.

He questions Liang about his folks, where they originate from, what they do, what amount of cash do they have? Liang's folks have very little, his mom fills in as a weaver, and his dad is an angler.

They can pay for Liang's training by carrying on with a cheap life. Zhu's dad expels him, guides him to return to class, and to discover a young lady in his own social class.

He disallows Zhu to have any more contact with Liang and advises his hirelings to ensure she doesn't go out solo.

Liang remains in the hotel, and he can't confront returning to class alone. He believes he needs to keep himself near Zhu. He lost his craving, and he essentially couldn't eat anything.

He sits at his window consistently, throughout the day, and watches out to check whether he can get a look at Zhu.

He became ill and pines away. Zhu can't escape the house, and the hirelings are not set up to ignore their lord.

She goes through her days, sobbing for her darling. One of the workers has offered to take messages to the motel and back. That is the way one dismal day she discovered that Liang had kicked the bucket.

Zhu cries to an ever-increasing extent, yet her folks continue with the arrangements for the wedding in any case. Her dad is sure that in the end, she will overlook this poor understudy, and will acknowledge her obligations as a decent girl and spouse.

However, Zhu doesn't quit crying; she cries and cries until every one of the tears in her body is spent. At that point, she begins crying blood, rather than tears; little pearls of blood leave her eyes. The day of the wedding shows up.

Zhu will be conveyed in a palanquin to her new spouse's home. She educates her bearers to take the course that passes the graveyard where Liang is covered.

At the point when they arrive, she arranges them to stop, and she gets out to state a supplication over his grave. As she bows somewhere around the grave, a butterfly shows up, and it appears as though it left Liang's grave.

It hovers around her head, and she watches it, entranced. She is certain this butterfly looks simply like her dead darling, Liang. She extended her arms towards the butterfly, which flies up somewhat, over her head.

She lifts her head and her arms towards it, and as the butterfly flies higher up, she understands that her arms have transformed into butterfly wings, and she can go along with him currently, finally, and together they fly away from this spot brimming with dead individuals.

Her workers come searching for her. However, they don't see anyone. Everything they can see is a couple of butterflies horsing around over the graves, at that point vanishing into the blue separation.

Remembering Easily

Contemplation and guided symbolism for unwinding can be utilized to accomplish objectives working with the subliminal personality to deliver the ideal outcomes. You can utilize guided symbolism to enable your youngster to comprehend everything that she's found out in school and throughout everyday life.

Practice this frequently and utilize positive attestations also to strengthen these thoughts, for example, "Your psyche resembles a library" and "You as of now have all the data within you." Use a quieting voice to lead the symbolism and unwind into the minute with your kid.

I'm going to share a little story.

Close your eyes and relax. Also, simply envision all that I'm stating. Take in a sweet, full breath, similar to you're going to victory birthday candles. Breathe in gradually, and afterward blow it out gradually and delicately. Presently take in, and afterward inhale out. Excellent!

We should imagine now that we're in a mansion. It's made of stone, and you see a major overshadow in the corner. We go to the pinnacle and discover an entryway. It's a monstrous, substantial entryway made of harsh wood.

At the point when you step into the pinnacle, you're at the highest point of a long winding staircase made of stone, and you see burns on the divider to light the way. The pinnacle feels cool. Walk around the stairs, realizing delightful things are directly here prepared for you to investigate.

Presently that you're at the base of the staircase, you see that there are a few rooms covered up underneath this pinnacle before you is a lobby, with entryways on each side that lead to singular rooms.

Go down the foyer and open the principal entryway to your right side. Inside, you see a little room filled from floor to roof with books. It's a whole library with a work area in the focal point of the room.

This room contains only a smidgen of the data that you hold in your mind. This room is a piece of you, so all that you've at any point learned or been instructed can be found here.

Each room contains an alternate subject, and as you keep on learning, these libraries will proceed to develop and develop with an ever-increasing number of books. Why not pull a book off the rack and glance through it? These libraries are a piece of you, and you can get all the data in these libraries in any event, when you're wide conscious!

You've taken in much more than you most likely figured it out! This is a spot you can come back to whenever you need, even in the center of a school day, or when stepping through a test or exam. You can just recall how you have everything previously put away inside you.

You essentially make sure to open the correct book mysteriously, and you'll recollect so effectively!

Set your books aside presently, realizing that you can get to them whenever you have to.

Stroll back up the stairs and venture out into the daylight!

You can open your eyes and squirm your fingers and toes.

Presently, you can return to your library whenever you have to in your creative mind!

Internal Realm

I am going to disclose to you an incredible story of a great domain.

Get yourself in an agreeable position. Close your eyes, and just envision that you are a piece of this story.

Breathe in an extreme breath and let it out gradually. As you keep on breathing profoundly and tranquility, consider something you progress nicely.

What do you truly love to do? This is called ability, and we as a whole have something that we're great at doing. Presently simply feel those nice sentiments of doing what you appreciate and keep on concentrating on your relaxing.

Feel yourself getting lighter and lighter. Take another breath, and feel yourself ascending up ever more elevated. Take another breath, and feel yourself ascending so high that it feels like you're drifting.

Keep your breathing consistent and quiet, while flying through the sky, skimming reporting in real-time. At the point when you're flying this way, if you need to go to a spot, you should simply consider it.

Consider a domain where everybody worships your ability. It's an extraordinary spot where everybody respects you so, especially for your remarkable capacity! You resemble the sovereign or ruler of that palace!

As you draw close to the château doors, you recognize a tremendous standard that says, "We love you!" All of the townspeople are arranged in the city with banners and flags, and they're all supporting you as you stroll toward the entryway. Everyone's yelling and saying, "No doubt about it!" "You're FANTASTIC!"

You stroll toward the entryway and head inside. A man in an interesting looking suit is remaining there to welcome you. "Welcome to our realm!" he says. "You're our new ruler! We've been hanging tight for you!"

This realm is where they truly cherish and appreciate individuals who can do all the magnificent things that you can do, and since you accomplish something so well, they need you to be the new leader of their realm!

Every one of the individuals loves you and wants to resemble you. You are a good example and motivation for everyone here! How can it feel knowing this? Maybe you have a monstrous sentiment of appreciation gushing in your heart! You can return to this realm whenever you overlook how stunning you are, and every one of the individuals here will remind you how staggering and astounding you are.

For the time being, it's an ideal opportunity to return home, yet you can convey all the excellent sentiments back with you and appreciate them consistently.

Presently, I'll reveal to you a mystery about this realm of yours. The individuals from your realm - the individuals who imagine that you're astonishing and great - are in reality surrounding you!

They're the only sort of dissipated in the waking scene, so you may need to search for them. Be that as it may, if you continue being wonderful and searching for those unique individuals, you'll discover many individuals around you who know the reality of how exceptional and delightful you genuinely are!

The Golden Axe

Let's breathe in and get completely relaxed. Let's get all warm and cozy in our bed.

Do you know that in the old times, electric and gas heaters and stoves didn't exist? Most people relied on firewood to stay warm during the winters. In those times, woodcutting was a separate profession, and some people earned only through cutting and selling wood.

One such person is the main character of our story today. His name was Jack. Jack's family was destitute. Him, his wife Delphia and his poor blind mother Mary lived in a small wooden hut at the edge of a thick forest. Mary's biggest wish was to have a little grandchild one day.

One day when Jack was cutting dried wood in the forest, he lost his axe. It really worried him, it was his only source of income after all. When he couldn't find his axe anywhere, he sat next to a tree in his agitation and began to cry.

Jack felt a hand on his shoulder and raised his head. Behold! It was a Fairy! She had deep blue wings and a golden magic wand.

"Hey, woodcutter! Why are you so gloomy today?" The fairy asked in a sweet voice.

"I... I have lost my wooden axe! It is not just a tool, but a dear friend too! How will I feed my family without any wood to sell", he bowed his head once again.

"Oh no worries, I will find your axe for you!" The fairy exclaimed excitedly.
The woodcutter looked up with hope.

The fairy disappeared; when she reappeared, she had a brilliant Golden Axe in her hands. "Is this your axe, oh hardworking man?"

"No, no" Jack replied immediately, "My axe is old, its wooden handle is worn and scratched, its iron head is rusty and blunt."

The fairy disappeared once again; when she reappeared this time, she had a shining Silver Axe in her arms. "Is this your axe, oh skilled woodcutter?"

"No, no, kind fairy!" Jack replied immediately, "My axe is not new and shining, but very old, its wooden handle is worn and scratched, not shiny or silver, its iron head is rusty and blunt, not brilliant or sharp."

The fairy disappeared yet again; she reappeared with an old, shabby wooden axe in her arms this time. Its handle was cracked and worn, and its blade was rusty and blunt. "Is this your axe, oh truthful, honest man?"

Jack's face lit up with delight at the sight of his own axe, "Oh yes, *yes*, that is indeed my own axe! How will I ever repay you, oh kind fairy?"

"My dear honest man, you don't need to repay me! I am the forest guardian, it is my duty to help anyone who needs assistance in this forest" The fairy smiled in response, "I will reward you for your honesty, tell me one special wish, and I will make it come true!"

Jack thought very carefully, his family had only three needs, they were destitute, his old mother was blind, and he didn't have children.

"I wish that..." Jack said very carefully "My mother would see her grandchild grow up in riches!"

And thus, Jack's wish came true brilliantly, Jack was given a job in the king's court, his mother gained her sight back, and Delphia and Jack became parents to a beautiful little girl. They named her Olivia. And Olivia's grandma watched her grow up in riches.

Hey, but our story doesn't end here!

When the fairy had presented Jack with the Golden and the Silver axes, someone had watched from the shadows. This was Daniel, Jack's greedy neighbor. But right before he could see the fairy presenting Jack with his own axe, Daniel had run away to plan his scheme.

Daniel went to the forest the next day. He sat down in a corner and began to weep. The fairy appeared in front of him and touched his shoulder. "Hey, gloomy soul! I've never seen you here before! Who would you be? And what makes you so sad?"

Daniel lied to the fairy, "I have lost my axe! How will I cut wood without it!"

"No worries, stranger!" The fairy responded in a sweet voice, "I will find your axe for you!"

The fairy disappeared; she reappeared a moment later holding the Golden Axe she had presented to Jack before, "Is this your axe stranger?"

"Yes, yes!" Daniel shouted in greed, "That is my axe, hurry, hurry, give it to me!"

But the fairy knew this was not Daniel's axe. She kept backing away, and Daniel kept following her. They reached in the middle of the forest.

Then the fairy disappeared in this air. Daniel got lost as a punishment for his greed. And it is said that he never found his way out of that forest. He became a forest sage and lived forever after in the middle of the thick forest.

Peaceful Retreat

Shut your eyes, and take in a good deep breath. Feel your entire body begin to relax with your calm, even breathing. Let your body get cozy and comfortable. If you need to change positions, go ahead and move to wherever or however feels right to you.

Take another big deep breath and release it gently.

We're going to use the power of our minds to go on a peaceful retreat. This will be a place you can visit any time you like - just by using your mind.

Let the whole of your imagination move you to a beautiful wooded area. Sunlight filters down through the thick leaves of tall trees. The air around you is perfectly comfortable - not too hot and not too cold.

It's a safe place, and everything around you is ripe for exploring. The air smells fresh, and as you pay attention to other scents, you notice the smell of moss and maybe even water nearby. You saunter through this playful, welcoming forest, looking all around at the beauty of nature. Small birds chirp and hop around the forest floor and flitter up to the trees.

There's an old fallen tree on the ground, and you watch as a squirrel darts inside to store an acorn. As you walk further, you hear the sound of gently flowing water. You follow the sound and the smell of freshwater. Then you see it. A crystal clear spring that flows down into a narrow stream.

You're drawn to the lightly flowing water. It looks so peaceful. So you sit on a big rock right beside the spring. The rock is warm from the sun, and as you stretch your legs down, your toes dip into the shallow, clear spring water. It feels so refreshing and relaxing. This spot feels like it was created, especially for you - your own personal retreat in the natural world.

Lean your head backwards and ensure to close your eyes as the leaves dance above you in the gentle breeze and little patches of sunlight and shadow move across your face. Doesn't it feel pleasant to be in this particular place?

The stream is continuously flowing - just like good things can always come into your life. And just as you can let worries go or fears by allowing them to float away downstream.

This place lives inside you. Anytime you want to visit it, you can simply come here in your mind. Stay here in your peaceful retreat for as long as you like.

You can open your eyes when you feel you are ready, and give your body a big stretch.

Marvelous!

You've done a fantastic job using your imagination.

Being Helpful

Today we will go on an undertaking in our psyches. It will feel unwinding and enjoyment simultaneously. In this way, when you are prepared, I was hoping you could close your eyes and tune in to the sound of my voice.

As you genuinely focus on each word, let your body loosen up to an ever-increasing extent. The calming sound of each word resembles an influx of unwinding that enters the highest point of your head and goes down your whole body.

It loosens up every single muscle. Your neck starts to feel extremely loose. Your jaw is agreeable, and even your eyes and temple start to relinquish any pressure or snugness. Your body enjoys a reprieve from all the morning's exercises and realizes it can rest be still for these minutes in flawless agreement and harmony.

The remainder of your body loosens up now - your shoulders, arms, chest, and now your belly, hips, and back. Your hands unwind, and even each finger - individually. The unwinding currently proceeds with its excursion down your upper legs, your knees, lower legs, into your lower legs, down to your feet, and into every single toe. Presently your body feels completely quiet and like you're coasting on a cloud.

As we start this day, we center on thoughtfulness and deciding to utilize our words tenderly - when we address ourselves as well as other people. We're going to focus on our considerations and guide them, such that makes us and others feel better. We do this since it feels better inside and makes a positive domain and an upbeat day! We feel much improved and experience more joy and goodness when we are caring with our words, considerations, and activities.

Today we additionally center on being useful to other people. Being a cooperative person is significant because it makes life more joyful, thus considerably more enjoyable! At the point when we help other people, the other individual advantages, obviously, however, we do, as well.

Helping others exhibits thoughtfulness in real life. Being useful implies that others realize they are not the only ones, and it lights up their day. Recall when somebody helped you. How did that cause you to feel? It was a great blessing. You can give a similar grace today and consistently by being benevolent and accommodating to others with words and activities.

Not every person is generally so kind and supportive. However, these are the individuals who need it the most. Perhaps, they have never had a case of benevolence or supportiveness, and from your model, they can decide to improve and be more joyful and kinder, as well.

Presently, when you're prepared, take in a full breath and take your consideration back to where you are.

You have made a phenomenal showing of unwinding and utilizing your splendid personality to consider things in new manners.

Along these lines, bring back every one of the sentiments of goodness and let them control you on this great day!

The Magical Pencil

Breath in deeply, now hold the air in your belly, like a balloon, now let it all go. Take a deep breath like this a few more times. Are you relaxed now? Let's begin.

One upon a time, in a small town called Cloudy. There lived a very skilled painter called Albert. Albert's paintings were so good that they looked almost real. Albert made paintings of the sunset, and of flowers and birds, and he made portraits of people. But since Cloudy was such a small town, soon he ran out of work.

There was a tree near the lake, where Albert used to sit, to paint the sunset. Albert always talked to the tree as if it were a person, it was after all, now a friend of Albert's, as he spent so much time here. Sometimes Albert felt as if the tree could understand what he said.

What Albert didn't know, was that the tree was home to a little fairy named Twinkle. Twinkle was very shy, so she never talked to Albert, but she really liked his paintings and always tried to encourage him in little ways like rustling the tree leaves when she thought he was tired.

When Albert told the tree about his troubles in finding work and how he might have to travel to some other town to find a job, it made Twinkle very sad. She really wanted to help Albert. She worked all night and made a special pencil for Albert. It was covered in shiny ribbons and had a pretty jewel on top of it. She placed the pencil very carefully at the base of the tree and waited for Albert to come and find it.

The next day when Albert went to his favorite tree, he found the most beautiful pencil at the base of the tree. At first, he got very excited and picked up the pencil, but then he realized that the pencil might belong to something else, he put it back down and went away. Twinkle sighed and shook her head.

The next day, when Albert found that the pencil was still there, he thought that pencil mustn't have any owner and thus, Albert could probably use it. He picked up the pencil and set up his canvas. With this pretty pencil, he drew a leaf.

But oh? What did he find? As soon as he was done drawing a leaf, a real leaf flew out of the paper and fluttered slowly to the ground. At first, Albert couldn't believe it! He decided to try one more time. This time he drew an apple. Right before his eyes, a bright red apple appeared out of the canvas and fell on the grass. Albert clapped his hands with delight. He took the pencil home with him.

When he reached home, he decided to draw a mango. But in his excitement, he could only draw a misshapen circle. Nothing appeared out of the paper. He tried again. But he was so jittery with excitement that he could only draw a shape like an egg. He realized that he had to be calm and composed, and draw a proper object, only then it would appear for real. So, he calmed himself and tried again. This time he drew a perfect mango, and it instantly appeared out of the canvas

Albert was now delighted; he could get whatever he wanted; all he had to do was draw it with the magical pencil. But only a few days passed, and Albert became bored with this new power. What would he work for, now that he could get anything he wanted? Then, a realization came over him! He decided he could give his friends, and all the people of Cloudy Town everything *they* needed too.

So he went to the Town square and told everyone that he could get them whatever they wanted. At first, everyone laughed at him. "Have you started telling stories now too? Ha Ha Ha", "Oh, you have a magic pencil, don't you? Ha Ha Ha Ha". But then Albert decided that he could just *show* them!

Albert knew his friend David needed a tractor for his farm. So he drew a picture of an adorable tractor and placed the paper on the road. And the townspeople witnessed as a full-sized tractor appeared in front of their eyes. Everyone applauded. Now they all believed him.

The people of Cloudy Town were all honest and straightforward, they never asked Albert for anything they didn't need. Soon, the little town became exceedingly prosperous, and tourists started to visit.

One of these tourists was a very greedy man called Weber. When he noticed how happy and content everyone in Cloudy Town was, he started to ask around. The simple-minded people of Cloudy told him the truth.

Weber decided to kidnap Albert, the painter. He hid behind Albert's house, and when the painter returned home in the evening, Weber caught by his arm, and threatened him, "Draw some rubies for me with your magical pencil and a bag to put them in! Hurry! Hurry!". Albert was so scared that all he could draw was some rocks.

Weber got angry and took the pencil from Albert's hand, "You're trying to trick me, YOU STUPID MAN! I'll draw it myself! I will draw a gold chain!". But you see, Weber wasn't good at drawing at all! So what Weber drew actually turned into a big scary snake!!

When Weber was trying to run away from the snake, Albert took over his fear and calmly drew a big cage. The cage fell on Weber and trapped him inside it. Albert ran to the police station and reported everything. The police officer came to arrest Weber and take him away to jail.

After this whole episode, Albert realized how dangerous such a pencil could be. He took the pencil to his favorite tree and buried it at the tree's base. It is said that in a small town named Cloudy, even today, a magical pencil is buried at the bottom of a tree, on the top of which a very shy fairy lives.

Paying Attention

Do you realize that within you, you have some thoughtful responses to every one of the inquiries you'll ever have about your life? It's valid.

Today, we will figure out how. Close your eyes and take in an exceptionally moderate, full breath. Presently, breathe out gradually. Continue breathing profoundly and feel the natural air come in through your nose and stream right down to your midsection. Feel your stomach stretch out as you take in.

Ensure your abdomen is going gradually in and out as you breathe in and breathe out.

Each time we inhale, we should attempt to inhale this way – permitting the air to go right down to the tummy – not merely in the lungs. This loosens up your entire body and keeps you feeling serene, regardless. It's additionally the correct method to relax.

Presently, as you keep on breathing profoundly, direct your concentration toward something different. I might want you to listen cautiously to all the peaceful sounds outside of you and happening surrounding you. You may hear outside commotions, possibly autos, winged animals, or something different... simply tune in to every one of the sounds – both blackout and noisy. (Respite)

Presently, how about we turn your concentrate internal.

Listen unobtrusively to what you hear occurring inside your body. Would you be able to listen to your heart, pulsating? (Delay)

Would you be able to hear your breath as you inhale gradually in and out? Possibly your stomach is in any event, making commotions. Whatever is going on inside, simply set aside an effort to listen cautiously. Just focus on the sound of your breath. It's practically enchanted. Your entire body is alive, and it's this breath, in addition to other things, that is keeping you alive.

Permit the breath to top off your entire body and appreciate as the living vitality of your breath goes into every single cell, every single iota of your body... feel that and loosen up further.

Presently listen much more intently... visit and focus if any emotions are coming up the present moment... sentiments within you that should be communicated or discussed. Our emotions reveal to us a great deal.

At the point when we are peaceful and quiet, we can take advantage of those emotions and listen far better. Possibly you'll out of nowhere find a solution to an inquiry you've had, or you will acknowledge something you have been feeling from the beginning.

We should set aside the effort to hear ourselves out every single day. It causes us to interface with who we indeed are inside and is an essential piece of growing up and realizing ourselves better.

In this sheltered, calm space we're in the present moment, you can without much of a stretch tune in to what's happening inside. Your considerations and emotions truly matter! You can confide in yourself and your sentiments.

Next time you have an inquiry on what you ought to do – simply approach and afterward tune in inside for your answer. Open your eyes when you're prepared and give your body a significant stretch.

Relaxing on A Beach

Our psyches are so imaginative and compelling that we can move ourselves to wherever we want, just by envisioning it in our brains. As the climate turns colder outside, we can, in any case, bring the warmth inside through our guided symbolism reflection this month.

We're going on an extraordinary experience to the sea. We are going to savor all the landscape, and peaceful the seashore brings to the table us!

Close your eyes and carry yourself to a quiet, calm spot in your psyche. Simply remain here and unwind for a couple of seconds.

Inhale profoundly and serenely and notice how stunning the sound of your breath is. Simply center and tune in to the air moving in and out... It is a serious alleviating and staggering sound.

Presently envision moving mysteriously to your preferred spot on a seashore. On the off chance that you have never been to a shore, simply envision what you figure it would resemble. Envision yourself there now.

On the seashore, you feel the lapping of the warm waves against your toes. You delve your toes profound into the cold, wet sand. The sun sparkles brilliantly and tenderly warm your skin. Maybe the sun is coming to down and pouring its adoration on you.... so warm thus stunning.

Feel the musicality of the tranquil waves streaming over the sand, loosening up you. Note how smooth and even your breathing has become. Breathe in and afterward breathe out gradually and smoothly. Presently you are hindering your breathing significantly further and permitting your muscles to unwind.

Feel the glow of the sun softening your muscles into complete unwinding. Gradually and quickly, your body loosens up to an ever-increasing extent, discharging strain or dissatisfaction, discharging any stresses or questions you have. Breathing in profoundly again - take in quiet and serenity. Your body is presently loose; your brain is loosened up now as well. You can purge your psyche all things considered or considerations that have been disturbing you. Simply appreciate this minute you have now.

Right now, this is the thing that issues just, unwinding and savoring this minute. Take in profoundly and permit the unwinding to stream to any piece of your body that requirements it.

Envision the lovely brilliant warm sun infiltrating every single cell and muscle, causing you to feel so excellent and alive! I'm sure you can feel the harmony that encompasses you currently, telling you that everything is okay.

Take in a beautiful, full breath again and take your consideration back to where you are... alongside all the quiet, tranquil sentiments of unwinding and rest. I realize you are feeling empowered and peaceful currently, prepared for a delightful night's rest.

This a decent time to talk about what your kid felt during the unwinding or any feelings of dread or stress that appear. Realize that your kid is in an exceptionally vulnerable state at present, so remaining positive, adoring things is the way to set up your kid's intuitive personality for progress!

The Cozy Castle

This evening, how about we go to an enchanted spot with our creative mind.

Simply close your delightful and stunning eyes and let your body to start to unwind.

We are setting off to a comfortable château high in the mists. Try not to regard it ordinary, and it is undoubtedly an uncommon and an otherworldly manner where dreams work out as expected, where we can unwind and simply appreciate some serene and agreeable minutes.

Imagine since you are coasting comfortably on a delicate white cloud. It feels astonishing just to rest and unwind here. Presently envision that the cloud carries you to the entryway of an excellent manor.

The main sound you hear is the calming snapping of the fire in the chimneys. It warms the entire palace, and you feel so fulfilled and beautiful here. There is an inclination of satisfaction and gloriousness in this spot. The whole château is loaded up with the alleviating smell of lavender, and it quiets you significantly more. You feel honored to be here and experience the glow and harmony in this spot.

Presently, stroll down the lobbies of this magnificent palace. Envision an entryway before you that appears to welcome you inside. A sentiment of welcome washes over you look into the room and see your name over a delicate cushion bed. The bed must be enchanted because as soon you plunk down on it... it invites you to fall once again into it and simply loosen up the entirety of your stresses away...

You can't consider whatever else at this moment, aside from how magnificent and quiet it feels here... how great you feel inside. You realize this is your extraordinary spot, and you can come here at whatever point you need, just by considering it.

You feel all your pressure and strain leave your body right away. Quiet, peaceful sentiments wash over you. This is your place of friendship. You realize that regardless of what's going on around you, you are welcome here to unwind and feel settled.

Look into now and notice a pleasant, splendid star evident in the sky, at that point, another. You understand you are lying on a delicate bed now under the open air. Before long, the smooth dark sky is wholly lit with sparkling stars like precious stones. The view is so excellent and tranquil that you can't take your eyes off the stars.

You may want to extend your hand and contact the sky. Check out it — who comprehends what can occur supernaturally. As you loosen up your grasp, shockingly, you can contact the stars.

Pick a star and mostly pluck it out of the sky — it's okay to do as such. As you look nearer, you understand a few etchings on the star. Stunning! It has your name on it. It refers to when you were a little anxious about something or felt worried by a circumstance, yet instead, you decide to confront your dread and handle the condition fearlessly.

The star you grasp was made to respect your accomplishment. A warm and shellfish whirlwind and pride overwhelms you. Every one of these stars is your accomplishments! You study the entire sky cautiously.

Such a large number of stars, such a significant amount of accomplishments! You guarantee yourself that you will keep on endeavoring to get these stars of greatness in the sky of your heart.

Feeling massive sentiments of harmony, quiet, and bliss topping off your central core, you calmly continue with your rest today around evening time.

By A Lakeside

In this contemplation, we will help children to liberate themselves from stress, distress, and stress. Build up a loosening up condition with diminishing lights and a delicate cover. You can even include loosening up mood melodies and diffuse fundamental lavender oil to make a mitigating environment. Breathe in a moderate, full breath and begin perusing with a mitigating, and delicate voice.

Take a full breath and shut your eyes gradually. Envision the scenes that I am going to let you know while you're despite everything breathing steadily and tranquility.

Envision yourself loosening up sitting by a large, calm lake.

The breeze delicately blows over the lake, and you watch the vast number of modest waves it makes on the outside of the lake. The surroundings here are so serene and respecting that it brings a sentiment of complete agreement that is cleared over your entire body and brain. You breathe in profoundly and let the harmony fill in you.

You are hearing flying creatures' delicate twittering and musical melodies of unadulterated satisfaction. Right now is an ideal opportunity to oust out any worry, any upsetting considerations, any distress you may be feeling. Let those sentiments skim up, out, and away.

Whatever has happened today that has annoyed you, the time has come to release that. Realize that you are indeed in charge of your psyche and your body. You can decide to permit these upsetting feelings to leave. In doing as such, you will free up space in your central core for positive what might be on the horizon.

Life is tied in with producing what you like and picking the correct feelings that cause you to feel great. At the point when you center on the positive, you get progressively positive encounters throughout your life. Discharging any negative considerations fills in as an umbrella on a stormy day – sure the downpour is there, yet it doesn't need to influence you.

In your oblivious personality – envision yourself now in a stormy, blustery condition. As you open up your umbrella of energy, you perceive how well-shielded you are from such's going on out there. You don't need to be a piece of the stormy issues. It is your decision on how to react to whatever comes in your direction.

Understand that you have every one of the abilities you need inside, simply decide to utilize them. You can picture your life from an upbeat point of view. Stress, upsetting considerations, or trouble are selections of thoughts you think, and you can fundamentally disapprove of them. Discharge every one of the things that have been distressing to you, and you can make harmony with yourself.

Make harmony now with the stunning individual that you are from inside. Support yourself with your caring contemplations. Discharge any negative pictures or thoughts you hold about yourself. You have a decision in what you accept, and your brain is your most prominent resource and your best apparatus.

Presently take in a decent full breath, let the serene and positive sentiments to top off your heart and psyche... tranquility and quiet encompass you from all over at this point.

Open your eyes when you are prepared.

Happy Breathing

Breathe in gradually yet profoundly, and close your delightful eyes.

Proceed with breathing this way and feel all the new and high air going into your nose and streaming right down to your tummy. Feel your stomach is extending out as you take in profoundly. Note how the breath feels to you as it delicately flows in through your nose, into your throat, and further and additionally down it goes to tummy.

Ensure your abdomen is moving gradually here and there as you breathe in and breathe out. Is it true that it isn't pleasant to feel this quiet and calm after the first dynamic day you've had? It's ideal for our bodies and our psyches just to feel this quieting breath streaming in and out. When we are figuring out how to concentrate on our breathing, we're rehearsing reflection.

Contemplation encourages our center, and it gives us harmony and a condition of serenity. Everybody needs to be quiet! Reflection is just being exceptionally engaged and peaceful inside. Presently right now, listen warily to all sorts of sounds outside and surrounding you.

You may hear outside clamors. You may tune in to autos, fowls, or maybe something different. It's splendidly, alright. We're merely figuring out how to focus... so simply tune in. (Interruption)

Presently, turn your concentrate internal. Listen carefully and unobtrusively to what's going on inside your body. Would you be able to hear your heart pulsating? (Delay)

Would you be able to hear your inward breath as you inhale continuously and calmly in and out? Possibly your stomach is making commotions; maybe everything is incredible, quiet. Whatever is going on inside, simply set aside the effort to listen cautiously and notice everything that is going on within. (Delay)

It is practically enchanted and offbeat to concentrate on the sound of your breath. Your whole body is alive and feels so great! You realize this breath is extraordinary. It's a piece of the vitality that streams all through us, and by working with our entire body, it keeps us feeling so great all around.

Permit the pure air to top off your whole body now and appreciate as the vitality goes into every single cell of your entity; and every single muscle of your lovely body. Envision that your upbeat breath is carrying a major beautiful grin to each place in your body. Does that vibe well?... It feels great to me!

Attempt to spend a tad bit of your day merely envisioning this. You will be truly astounded at how superb it will cause you to feel everywhere.

Presently when you're prepared, you can open your eyes and give your body a significant stretch.

You've worked superbly, and I can simply envision all that bliss you've spread wherever in your body.

I'm incredibly pleased with you for your reflection today!

Kindness Conquers

Do you know the world's strongest emotions are happiness and love? Nothing can bring change faster than Kindness can! Today let's enjoy a story that proves just that.

In a small village at the bank of a river, there lived a poor fisherman. The fisherman was a very kind and loving man, while his wife was a perfect looking woman. They had a very pretty little daughter called Leanna.

One day when the fisherman went to the river to catch some fish, he witnessed a strange sight. He saw a baby girl floating in the river on a large leaf! He carefully picked up the beautiful little girl and took her home. His wife became furious when she saw the little girl, as they were destitute and she was worried that they wouldn't be able to raise two little girls instead of one.

The fisherman named the little girl Fiona and raised her as his daughter just like Leanna.

Years passed, and both little girls grew up into two lovely young women. Where Leanna was beautiful like her mother, Fiona was very kind and sweet like her father.

After the fisherman passed away though, the mother really started hating Fiona, she always called Fiona unfortunate for the family.

Fiona was given very little food, and she had to do all the housework too. And she had to walk a mile away to fill the water pots.

One day when she was filling the water pots at a fountain, Fiona started crying. She lifted her head when she felt a hand on her shoulder, it was an old woman smiling down at her.

"My dear girl, would you give me some water? I'm very thirsty."

"Oh, of course, dear lady, here."

Fiona held her water pot up, as the old woman drank the water.

"My dear child, you are very kind, I will reward you for your kindness", the old woman said, "Every time something touched your heart or makes you cry, precious gems will fall from cheeks instead of tears", saying this, the old woman turned into a beautiful fairy and touched her sparkling magical wand to Fiona's head and disappeared in sparkling smoke.

Fiona returned home happily.

But as she entered the house, her mother was outraged because she was very late, she shouted at Fiona, "Where on Earth were you? Go, cook some food, my poor daughter is dying of hunger!"

"Yes, mother", mumbled Fiona as she ran to the kitchen. She dropped to her knees in the kitchen and began to cry.

Tiny rubies and small diamonds fell from her cheeks, as promised by the fairy. When the mother entered the kitchen to witness this sight, she asked Fiona how this could be! Fiona told her mother everything.

The mother hurried to call Leanna and instructed her to go to the fountain to get water the next day.

"And when you see an old woman asking for water, very kindly give her water, alright?" She told Leanna.

Leanna listened to every word carefully. She took the most beautiful silver pot and left for the fountain.

When Leanna was filling the beautiful silver pot with water, she saw an elegant young lady walking towards her from the forest.

"Oh, pretty young lady, could you please offer me some water, I am awfully thirsty", she asked Leanna.

"Oh, I'm here to pull pots of water from the fountain for *you,* am I?", Leanna replied rudely, "Oh, you must think anyone holding such a nice pot must be there only for you, Huh?"

The lady suddenly turned into a fairy, "I curse you for your rudeness! Now, every time you talk, only a frog's croaks will come out!"

When Leanna tried to stop the fairy, she could only croak. Leanna ran home, crying.

When her mother asked what was wrong, Leanna could only croak in response. The mother blamed Fiona for this and told her to go to the garden and tend to the plants.
As Fiona was cutting woods, she started to sing.

Unknown to Fiona, a prince was passing by, a little way away from her house.
As the prince listened to Fiona, he instantly fell in love with her. He asked his guards to ask who's house it was.

The mother came out of the house and told Leanna to go dress as Fiona before coming out.

As the prince looked at Leanna, he said, "My dear lady, your voice was so angelic, I couldn't help but fall in love, I would be honored to have you as my life partner. It would make me extremely delighted to hear you sing once again."

In her excitement, Leanna tried to sing, but she could only croak.

"Lady! What is this? Are you insulting me?" The prince shouted in anger, "Guards, arrest her!"

But before anyone could move, Fiona ran out of the house and called out to the prince, "Your Highness, please forgive my poor sister, she has been cursed, she cannot talk, please don't increase her hardships, even more, the one who was singing in the garden was really me!"

The prince did not want to be fooled again, so he requested, "Could you please sing for me then, dear lady".

Fiona began to sing, "Oh, dear prince, please do forgive my sister, she has been cursed and cannot speak, but she is ever so beautiful."

Hearing Fiona's sweet song for her sister, the fairy lifted the curse from Leanna.

The prince replied, "Oh, my dear lady, I will consider it my greatest honor if you were to accept my marriage proposal."

"Oh no, your highness", Fiona replied, "Please, it is my sister's dream to marry a prince and become a princess, please marry her instead."

"My dear lady, your kindness has made me fall in love even more, but there's no worry, as I have a little brother and he would surely accept lady Leanna as his wife!"

Both the young ladies married the princes and became princesses.

Soon elder Prince and Princess Fiona had a baby princess of their own. When she cried for the very first time, little pearls fell down her cheeks, becoming a living proof that kindness always conquers.

Feeling Loved

You are cherished!

This evening, I will reveal to you an astonishing story.

Loosen up your body in an agreeable position. At that point, close your eyes.

Presently imagine that you are the piece of the story. Breathe in all the high and clear air in you, and when you breathe out, feel everything that is encompassing you getting tranquil and quieter.

Take in another long breath, discharge it gradually, and feel much increasingly loose. As you keep on breathing profoundly and smoothly, notice that the main thing you need to focus on is my alleviating voice.

Presently envision a film screen before you. On the screen, you see pictures from your own life; when you accomplished something kind for somebody, or when somebody accomplished something bravo. As you watch the film, you perceive how satisfied you have made others, and you see all the happy-happy occasions when you were satisfied and happy also.

As you keep on watching this motion picture, you see when you helped someone who required you. You witness him getting upbeat after your guide. Simply this idea causes you to feel warm and fluffy inside.

Presently change to when somebody helped you. Consider how great you felt to realize that somebody was there for you when you required assistance. Feel each one of those lovely and beautiful sentiments return racing to your heart! Watch these fascinating snapshots of your life. Be mindful of how satisfied you were and how fantastic you felt! All these glad sentiments - each one of those occasions, you felt warm and fluffy - were a result of an outstanding inclination called love.

These things you find before you happened because you adored and demonstrated that affection to another person and because they love you. Love is tied in with dealing with others, doing extraordinary things, offering your thanks, and giving grace and tolerance. We are no different from inside – we are LOVE! That is indeed what our identity is!

At the point when we can express this piece of ourselves consistently, however much as could be expected... our hearts are topped off with delight and such fulfillment that occasionally we believe we may erupt from unadulterated satisfaction! Also, that cheerful love feeling implies that you're a piece of a network of individuals, an essential part of a caring universe!

I need you to recollect this adoration you have within you and how effectively you can express your affection with simple demonstrations of consideration towards yourself as well as other people. You are genuinely great. You are unadulterated love!

Love resembles a delicate, fluffy cover which folds us from all around. It causes you to feel warm, serene, and upbeat.

Presently take in a pleasant full breath and breathe out gradually. Keep on feeling all the beautiful sentiments of affection and delicacy as you cuddle in for rest this evening.

Sweet dreams!

One's Light

Delicately close your eyes now and delicately rehash, "I am still."

Notice your body unwind in a flash and quickly. Give your body to sink access your sleeping pad further and further, as your muscles become delicate and free. It feels so loose. Your body just appears to loosen up increasingly more with every single word you hear.

Presently envision a little shimmer of light somewhere profound inside your heart. This modest shimmer starts to shine more brilliant now, and you feel it coming to up and growing out. The shine turns out to be progressively distinctive, topping off your chest. You think the glow is spreading out contacting your stomach, your shoulders... getting more significant and more prominent... getting more splendid and more brilliant, sparkling right down to your toes.

Presently since your whole body sparkling like a brilliant star. This artificial light is your light - your sparkling light - your brightness. It is all the adoration in your heart. It is every one of your conceivable outcomes - and your choices are unending.

Sparkle your light any place you go. Sharing your view satisfies others, and it fulfills you too. It's a delightful inclination to share your light, and this way, you become a great guide to them.

At the point when you let this light of yours sparkle brilliantly, it tells others that they can likewise glimmer their incoming light splendidly. At the point when we as a whole do this, it makes the world an increasingly excellent, tranquil spot. Sharing your view is very like sharing your delightful grin or doing a carving demonstration.

Hold a glad idea about somebody, or send an upbeat wish to somebody who is feeling pitiful. It can mean helping somebody more youthful than you, or not as reliable as you. The entirety of this is sparkling your light, and you will find a wonderfully warm, fluffy inclination inside your heart when you do this. This remarkable inclination originates from doing what you were made to do – feeling and spreading adoration and happiness.

Sharing your light methods sharing the genuine you and being who you in reality are. It implies going to bat for the privilege and settling on decisions that vibe right to you in your heart.

Presently, let that brilliant light of yours to become like a quiet shower of firecrackers. Perceive how staggering and astounding you are as you light up the sky with your sparkling firecrackers.

As the firecracker sizzle and charge down, envision your beautiful light contacting the core of each individual you know and will meet. They feel more joyful because they know you. How beautiful and favored life is!

Presently I'd like for you to take in a full breath and bring back all the beautiful sentiments you have right now with you as you gradually stretch your body.

Open your eyes when you're prepared. You have worked admirably!

The Monkey King

Two voyagers were experiencing outside land together. They were reasonably bizarre travel friends since one of them couldn't come clean and could just glaringly lie. In contrast, the other couldn't lie regardless of whether his endurance relied upon it, and could only talk reality consistently.

They went for quite a while until they went to a place that is known for the monkeys. The King of the monkeys discovered that two outsiders had landed in his realm, and he was exceptionally anxious to intrigue them with his brilliance and quality, so he requested them to be brought before him.

He organized to get them situated on his royal position in his stateroom, in his royal residence and had an enormous entourage of subjects and hirelings arranged in long columns, both inside the room and along every one of the entries in transit in. As they advanced towards the stateroom, the explorers were very anxious, and they bowed when they preceded the ruler.

The ruler invited them generously and afterward inquired as to whether they'd at any point been within sight of a mightier lord. The explorer who consistently lied talked first. "Sire, I have voyage everywhere throughout the world, and at no other time have I been so intrigued by the quality and might of your court!" The lord appeared to be very satisfied to hear this, and he solicited, "And what's your opinion of my subjects?"

"O, lord of monkey," answered the lying explorer, "Your subjects must be the very blessed individuals I have met in the entirety of my broad ventures, sufficiently fortunate to be governed by such a grand and powerful decision ruler as you seem to be!

"The King of the Monkeys was incredibly satisfied with this answer, applauded and called upon his workers to set up an eminent dining experience for this uncommon visitor and to guarantee that every one of his needs was dealt with.

At that point, after that, he went to the next voyager and asked him a no different inquiry. This was, obviously, the explorer who could just talk reality through his eyes, so he stated, "O Lord, I think you are a little chimp, and every one of the subjects you rule over is superb gorillas, as well!

The ruler of the monkeys was angry after hearing this, and he hopped from his position of authority. He requested his gatekeepers to hold onto the hapless explorer and to pound the life out of him.

Stunning Dragonfly

Take in a profound unadulterated air inside you, and tenderly shut your eyes. Permit your belly to top off as far as possible up and afterward breathe out gradually. Do this progressively multiple times to loosen up your entire body truly.

You'll see how your body starts to feel profoundly loose and sinks further and further. Your legs begin to feel substantial. Your arms currently start to feel overwhelming and entirely agreeable. You appreciate each minute as your body keeps on feeling delicate and warm with each word I state.

Envision you're a delightful dragonfly shuddering about the sky. You see the beautiful green valley beneath you with heaps of bright blossoms, simply hanging tight for you to appreciate. You feel the breeze blow against your fragile, lacewings.

As the cold wind touch you, it bit by bit overwhelms any feelings of trepidation or any anxieties you feel. Appreciate how awesome it feels to be free. Your brain is so bright and quiet, and you are in absolute serenity. You look shocking when you permit your genuine satisfaction to radiate through you.

Gliding on the tranquil breeze seems to remind you that you can feel this way whenever you want. We all experience moments where we think big emotions, and that's ok. Emotions and feelings are meant to be explored. We can savor and hold on to these happy feelings as much as we want.

When a scary or angry emotion comes up, it's best to feel it and understand what it's here to teach us. Then we can let it go, so it doesn't stay trapped inside our minds or our bodies. As you continue flying like a stunning, magnificent dragonfly, note how the sun hits your body and also warms you up.

The big and puffy clouds floating in the sky are a reminder of how relaxed and calm you can be anytime you want, just by imagining it. We all experience many emotions every day. There is nothing wrong with them.

You can manage those substantial feelings by breathing profoundly, or gradually checking to 5, or working things out with somebody you trust. These are basic approaches to remain quiet, in any event, when we feel firm about something.

The earth is an interwoven of shading, and you appreciate every minute here as a dragonfly, floating along feeling so blissful and serene. You spread your wings far and stretch your body. It feels so great, and now you are prepared for an excellent day.

Take in a full breath now, and breathe out gradually.

At the point when you feel that you are prepared to open your eyes — give your body a significant stretch and open your eyes gradually and gradually.

Very much done! You've made an impressive showing picturing and unwinding.

Where Happiness Is Made

Close your eyes and envision coasting to a restrictive, quiet spot... a spot where you love to be. Skimming and coasting, as you have quite recently, let your body and mind rest and turn out to be extremely quiet.

Presently envision going into a beautiful nursery loaded with sweet-smelling roses and lilies. You stroll past the blossoms, contacting them gently to feel their delicate, fragrant petals. Out of nowhere, you see an excellent glancing working out yonder.

There is, by all accounts, nobody close or inside the structure. You contact the door handle, and the entryway opens only for you. Do you see a wide range of controls are found and think about what the sign on the divider says? Welcome to the spot name: "where satisfaction is made." Is it extremely conceivable to make joy?

You glance around and locate the main switch that you choose to flip on. You hear the messiness of machines folding without hesitation. You can see the entire apparatus and sequential construction system through a huge glass window. You see, a considerable container begins its excursion on a belt. A machine drops down to include something. You attempt to look inside and view, it was adding liberality to the container. Another gadget includes Sharing; one more includes love and afterward, goodness.

These characteristics are combined with a goliath whisk. Presently the container is moved to another belt. It moves to a place where it is steamed with Kindness. At the point when it leaves the chamber, it is chilled off with heaps of grins. Persistence and supportiveness are sprinkled on top.

You see that satisfaction can be made. Not by things outside of us or the kinds of stuff we purchase in a store. Instead, happiness is made when we do and express beautiful things, and when we are useful and liberal. Satisfaction is made when we share with others and love one another. This has been such a beautiful sight to see today!

Presently you know the key to assembling bliss! You keep this information in your heart, and you additionally share it with each possibility you get. Sharing what you have realized likewise causes satisfaction to develop.

Presently you rest easy as you stroll back outside and plunk down in a lovely, comfortable seat in the nursery. There is a great deal of bliss all around here, and within you, as well.

Whenever you feel somewhat miserable, you can make sure to open your container of satisfaction. You will begin to feel the entirety of the glow and positive sentiments that are quietly sitting tight for you to share!

Open your eyes now when you are prepared. Take in a drawn-out full breath and stretch your body.

A True Companion

Who don't we talk about friendship, today?

Do you know about two companions who set on a journey together, but one abandons the other?

Close your eyes and inhale all the good air in you. Let's begin our story of these companions.

Two travelers had been on a long journey through the countryside for many days. They took a walk along a track at the edge of a forest, when, some slightly ahead of them, they abruptly spotted a huge bear strolling towards them. They weren't sure if the bear had seen them, however they didn't want to take any chances.

The first traveler climbed the first tree he saw and hid among the tall branches. The second one dumped his bags and dropped to the ground, implying to be dead. He had heard once that bears don't really like to eat dead meat, so he hoped it was his safest way of surviving.

The bear approached the spot where the man was lying on the ground, who kept himself as still as he could, and did his best to hold his breath in. The bear sniffed all over his head for a few minutes, but did not seem to be interested in him at all, and went on his way. The second traveler cautiously ascended down from the tree to meet his friend. "Phew!" he said, "That was very close. From the tree, I could have sworn that the bear was talking to you!"

"Yes, it was actually talking to me", the second one replied. "He told me to be more cautious in the future when gong on a journey, and avoid to travel with anyone who backs out at the first sign of trouble!"

So, you know, a companion in need is a companion indeed.

That's what true companionship is.

Now, you should take a deep breath, close your eyes and go to sleep.

Goodnight!

Happy Heart

Take in a decent full breath, and close your eyes. We are going on a mysterious excursion inside! Did you realize you are so stunning you can go anyplace you need - just by utilizing your creative mind? That is the way uncommonly capable you are.

Today how about we bring an excursion into our hearts – a remarkable, excellent spot. There are times when we may feel pitiful or down, and that is alright. Whenever we feel on edge, we can check in with our hearts. We can decide to encircle ourselves with delightful sparkling light to bring ourselves comfort during troubling occasions.

As a matter of first importance, you may consider it to be daylight warm, relieving, unwinding to your body and brain. It may be splendid and foggy. Breathe in it profoundly, and let it quiet and solace you. Note how this gives you a feeling of harmony. Enjoy the warm, sparkling light that encompasses your body. Notice now as the fire goes to delicate blue, similar to the shade of the sky on a bright, marvelous day.

The delicate blue loosens up you and gives you significantly more harmony. You may begin to feel like you're floating on a cloud. Delicately and tenderly, the light is currently changing into a pinkish tint. Pay a unique mind to what it does. Accept a full breath as you permit the light pink shading to stream delicately into your body and stream legitimately into your heart.

Feel the delicate light removing the entirety of your damages. It causes you to relinquish distress and stress as you breathe out. Focus on the way that as you breathe out any horrendous emotions, agony, or bitterness, your heart starts to feel lighter and somewhat more liberated. The delicate, delicate light occupies space inside your heart and washes out any distress or agony. See the subtle, gleaming light filling much space in your heart... tenderly, productively, and affectionately. Inhale this quietness profoundly into all aspects of you, and notice the quiet and stillness dominate.

You can feel your life better because your heart feels better at this point. What's more, these feelings and sentiments will go with you the entire day. You can generally depend on this brilliant light to help you whenever you need it.

Envision your heart presently pulsating with joy, bouncing with euphoria and enthusiasm at what number of excellent individuals and extraordinary things encompass you. Life is so acceptable, and you feel tranquil.

Pause for a minute to feel appreciated through the adoration and couldn't care less that encompasses you. It's so stunning. Feeling quiet and serene currently, turn your consideration back to this room and your day - realizing that harmony is entirely yours.

At the point when you are prepared, give yourself a significant stretch and open your eyes if you feel like it. Or then again loosen up the remainder of your way into a tranquil rest.

The Pot of Roses

Let's get as comfortable as we can, and let's take in a deep breath. Let's begin our adventure for tonight.

In a deep magical forest, a long time ago, there lived an enchantress, the Forest Queen. The Forest Queen had a very dear friend, called Breanna.

When Breanna became the mother of a lovely baby girl, she invited the Forest Queen to visit her at her palace.

But as the Forest Queen was travelling towards Breanna's palace, something terrible happened! A cruel wizard attached the Forest Queen and her young prince Anthony.

The Forest Queen fought bravely, she left her son in the care of her dear friend Breanna and asked her to run away with him and her little daughter, so that the prince may stay safe until he reaches twenty-one years of age, and thus inherit all of the enchantress's powers.

Many years have passed since this mighty magical battle. Now let us travel to a small village, surrounded by a thick forest. Where in a small hut, there lived a destitute old farmer.

When the farmer's last days arrived, he called his son Stephan and his daughter Ella. He explained, "My dear children, I cannot give you a lot of things in inheritance, I don't really have anything besides that hen and the garden, a few stools and a silver ring. So I will divide what I have between you. My dear Ella, you can have this silver ring, and the pot of roses", he handed Ella the ring and pointed towards the pot of roses places on the windowsill, "And Stephan can have everything else", there were the last words of the dying old man.

Stephan laughed at his sister and cruelly told her that she cannot have anything from him and that she'll have to fend for herself.

The rudeness from her brother made Ella very sad. She looked at the pot of roses, and talked to the pretty flowers, "From now on, you are my only friends, I will take care of you, and tend to you", then seeing that the petals were drying, she added, "Hey, are you thirty? Let me get you some water!"

Ella ran and ran to get some water for her roses. At the edge of the forest, she found a battered down Villa, inside the villa, there was a fountain. She filled her watering can from the fountain.

As she was filling her watering can, Ella heard voices coming from inside the villa, she peeked from behind the wall to see a table in the garden. An elegant lady was sitting in front of the table. "Do come in, dear" the lady called to Ella. Ella was suddenly embarrassed. "Oh, I'm terribly sorry, I didn't mean to spy", Ella apologized. "Oh it's alright dear, I know you weren't spying." The elegant lady smiled at Ella, "I'm the Queen of this Forest, and I want to invite you to have lunch with me". Ella was shocked at this invitation, yet how could she decline the Queen of the Forest? She agreed to have lunch with the Queen.

After she'd had lunch, Ella thanked the Queen and said, "Your Highness, I don't really have anything to give you as thanks for the amazing lunch you shared with me, but there's a pot of roses that is the most precious thing in my life, I would like to present you with it", the Forest Queen smiled as she answered, "My dear Ella, you don't need to give anything as thanks, but since it is your choice to give me something so precious to you, I will accept it with gratitude."

The Queen's response made Ella very happy, so she hurried to her house to get the flower pot. As she reached her home though, Ella was shocked to see that her pot of roses was not on the windowsill where she had left it, instead there was cabbage in a pot sitting in its place.

Ella ran back to the Forest Queen and told her how her brother must've taken her pot of roses. She presented the Queen with her silver ring. The Queen told Ella not to worry. And that she will return to visit Ella when the twenty-first sun rises.

Ella was so worried for the poor roses that she became furious at the cabbage, and she picked it up to throw it out of the window. But hey! What's this? The cabbage spoke!

It pleaded with Ella to not throw it away, but plant it back in the cabbage patch, then it would tell Ella that her brother Stephan had hidden the pot of roses under his bed.
Ella ran to the vegetable patch and planted the cabbage back in the ground. Then she ran to Stephan's bedroom and took the pot of roses from under the bed. She watered them and placed them back on the windowsill.

When Ella came back from the window, she was shocked to see a chicken inside the house! She told the chicken to go back to the chicken shed. But hey! The chicken spoke too! It said it was freezing in the chicken shed that's why she came in here.

Ella asked the chicken how she could speak? And come to think of it, how could that cabbage speak? The chicken replied, "Oh, we can't usually speak! This must be a sign of the twenty-first sun!"

Ella was surprised to hear of the "twenty-first sun" again and asked the chicken what that meant.

The chicken began, "Oh well, a long time ago, when I used to be a woman, there came an exquisite lady to our old house. She brought a very pretty little baby girl with her. I had never seen such a beautiful baby in my life! And I had seen many babies since I was a nurse.

All she wanted to make the little poor girl to grow up in a poor farmer's house so that the evil wizard couldn't find her. She also gave us a silver ring and a pot of pretty roses. She told us that the little girl should inherit these two things from us. You must have realized that the little girl was you! Only I knew the secret of the Forest Queen, so she turned me into a chicken!". As the chicken was finishing her tale, the sun started to rise.

When the sun had appeared entirely, the Forest Queen appeared. She put a hand on Ella's shoulder as she spoke to her, "My dear Ella, as you have already heard the whole story from the old nurse, I'm here to take you away now". "But your Highness, why is the evil wizard looking for *me*?", Ella asked. "That is because my dear, your love and care protected my dear son, Prince Anthony! This rising sun is the son of his twenty-first birthday, today he inherits all my powers, and the evil wizard cannot hurt anyone anymore!".

"The prince was protected by *my* love and care? But how? Since I have never met the prince!".

"Oh, of course, my dear, you have cared for him and loved him more than anything else!". And as Ella watched, her precious pot of roses turned into a handsome Prince. "This is Prince Anthony, my dear, I had turned him into a pot of roses and left him in your care. Now he would like to accept you as his wife, the future Queen of the Forests!"

Prince Anthony and new wife Ella lived happily ever after and ruled the Forests for many years to come.

Did you know? The Prince's name, *Anthony,* comes from the Greek word *Anthos* which means *Roses.*

CPSIA information can be obtained
at www.ICGtesting.com
Printed in the USA
BVHW051920080421
604475BV00011B/1244

9 781801 943802